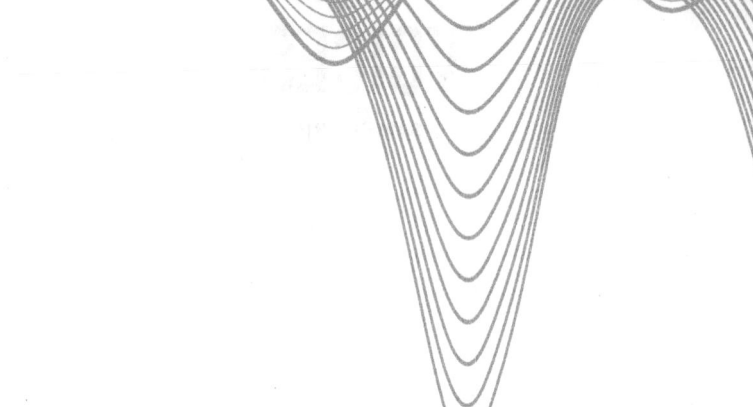

Copyright © 2024 by Sam Chand

Published by AVAIL

All rights reserved. No portion of this book may be reproduced, stored in a retrieval system, or transmitted in any form or by any means—electronic, mechanical, photocopy, recording, scanning, or other—except for brief quotations in critical reviews or articles, without prior written permission of the author.

All Scripture quotations are taken from the Holy Bible, New International Version®, NIV®. Copyright © 1973, 1978, 1984, 2011 by Biblica, Inc.™ Used by permission of Zondervan. All rights reserved worldwide. www.zondervan.com. The "NIV" and "New International Version" are trademarks registered in the United States Patent and Trademark Office by Biblica, Inc.™

For foreign and subsidiary rights, contact the author.

Cover design by Todd Petelle
Cover photo by Andrew van Tilborgh

ISBN: 978-1-962401-65-4   1 2 3 4 5 6 7 8 9 10

Printed in the United States of America

VOICES

The Power, Pain, & Purpose of Voices

SAM CHAND

AVAIL

Contents

CHAPTER 1. Voices We've Heard..........................7

CHAPTER 2. Voices We've Ignored.......................31

CHAPTER 3. Voices of Toxic Messages....................45

CHAPTER 4. Voices We Long to Hear 63

CHAPTER 5. Micro-Voices 81

CHAPTER 6. Competing Voices...........................95

CHAPTER 7. Screening the Voices 119

CHAPTER 8. Questioning Voices 133

CHAPTER 9. Tailoring Your Voice........................165

CHAPTER 10. Use Your Voice for Good 193

Endnotes..209

CHAPTER 1

Voices We've Heard

IN 1974, WHEN I WAS A STUDENT AND HAD ONLY BEEN in America a short while, I was attending a church near our college. I always sat in the back, but the pastor, Tom Grinder, noticed me. Before each service, he stood in the foyer greeting people until the last minute. At the exact moment the service was scheduled to start, he came through the doors and walked down the aisle to the platform to welcome people. At a midweek service on a Thursday evening, as I sat peacefully in the back row, Pastor Grinder opened the door, but he stopped

VOICES: The Power, Pain, & Purpose of Voices

as soon as he came in. He tapped me on the shoulder, looked into my eyes and said, "Sam, today you're going to lead the singing." Evidently, the regular song leader couldn't make it that day. Pastor Grinder didn't wait for my response. He just turned and walked quickly down the aisle.

I would have objected. I would have argued with him. At least I would have said, "Let me pray about it." I would have found a way to keep hiding in the back row, but he didn't give me any of those options. I got up and walked to the front of the church. After he greeted the crowd, he said, "Sam Chand is leading our singing tonight." That was my cue. I only knew a few songs. I quickly found them in the songbook, and I led the congregation in singing. Yes, in the 1970s, we sang from a songbook. We called it a *hymnal!*

I have no idea what prompted Pastor Grinder to tap me on the shoulder. He had never heard me sing, and in fact, I'd never led worship singing at a church. I'm sure it was a risk for him to ask me to lead that night, and I'd give a lot of money to have a video of my performance. (I'd pay for it so I could destroy it!) It was the first time someone asked me to take any leadership role, the first time someone believed in me, the first door that opened for me to impact people. He had observed enough about me to form an opinion that I needed an opportunity. Becoming the song leader was probably the last role I could have imagined, but Pastor Grinder was willing to take the chance. It all began with a tap on my shoulder. That moment began my platform service which continues to this day.

At crucial junctures, some wonderful people have stepped into my life with powerful, affirming voices to believe in me when I didn't see any reason to believe in myself. But I vividly remember a single derogatory word that forged my identity as a child.

When I was in the first grade in India, I was a rambunctious kid. I remember stepping on top from desk to desk across the room. I'm sure I exasperated my teacher, Miss Boniface. One day, she looked at me as I walked across the top of the desks and sighed, "Samuel, you are just a *janvar*." In Hindi, the word means "animal." I'm sure she didn't mean any harm. She wasn't yelling or clenching her teeth at me, but for the rest of my years in that elementary school, the name stuck. From that day on, students and teachers called me *janvar*, and I lived up to my moniker. The word defined me and gave me an identity. I acted like an animal because that's what people expected of me, and I spent many hours in the principal's office. I didn't devote myself to being a good scholar, and I didn't spend my energies on sports. I picked fights every day. I never won a fight—not one. In fights, I scraped, clawed, bit, and kicked. The fights really never ended because I started them again the next day. In fact, I fought with the same people day after day all year. My life revolved around being as disruptive as I could be so that I could validate others' opinions of me. Everybody wants to be known for something, and acting like an animal immediately became my USP—my "unique selling point." A single word can devastate us.

> I knew, though, that this statement had the potential to change my life.

Words can also have a wonderful, inspiring effect. Many years later, I had shed my identity as an animal to become an academician. I was president of Beulah Heights University, and I learned to be effective at administration, vision casting, and building relationships. One day, however, a man I respected looked me in the eye and said, "Sam, you are a really good leader." To be honest, I was very surprised by his comment because

I had never seen myself as a leader. My curriculum in Bible college and seminary didn't have a single course on leadership, and I wasn't even sure what a leader was. I knew, though, that this statement had the potential to change my life. This man's sincere affirmation meant the world to me, and the fact that he qualified the word "leader" with "really good" gave me a new standard to live up to. From that day forward, I saw my role in a different light. It wasn't that I changed directions or careers, but now I viewed myself and my role through a broader lens, and I had confidence that God could use me in bigger ways. My friend hadn't made an appointment that day to tell me how he saw me, and he wasn't playing the role of a life coach or mentor. He was just a trusted friend who held up a mirror to affirm what he saw in me, and he encouraged me deeply.

CONFLICTING VOICES

We can hear voices that communicate opposite messages on any given day (and often in the span of only minutes). For instance:

"You're really smart."

"Why aren't you as sharp as (a family member, a friend, or another leader)?"

"I've grown so much since I've joined your organization."

VOICES: The Power, Pain, & Purpose of Voices

"Why are you so stuck in the past?"
"You believe in me and make me feel more confident."
"You bring out the worst in me."
"I love you."
"I can't stand you."

How many of these comments does it take to cause damage? Not many.

The stark contrast in these voices can make us feel like we're losing our minds! If you've been in leadership longer than a week or two, you've undoubtedly heard at least a few people share horror stories about how their parents treated them. Adults can vividly remember parents' comments from decades before, like, "You'll never amount to anything," "I hate you! I wish we'd never had you," "You've ruined my life," "Get out of my face," "Why can't you be more like your sister?" and many others that crush a child's heart. How many of these comments does it take to cause damage? Not many. Words like these are inevitably coupled with contempt and devastating non-verbal messages of scowls, clenched teeth, and head shaking in disgust.

SIMILAR BUT DIFFERENT VOICES

Have you played pickleball yet? You probably will. It's the fastest-growing sport in America. The Association of Pickleball Professionals (Yes, there is one!) reported a startling rise from 5 million to 36.5 million players in a single year![1] (There's even a restaurant with pickleball courts in Houston. It's called Chick N Pickle.) Many of us have played other racquet sports, like tennis and paddleball, and we assumed our skills would easily translate to the new game. Wrong!

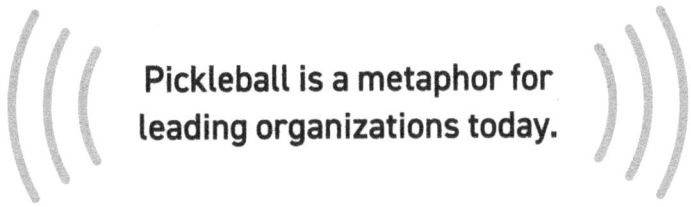

Pickleball is a metaphor for leading organizations today.

The equipment looks similar, but it's different.

The scoring is similar, but it's different.

The layout of the court looks similar, but it's different.

The strokes look similar, but they're different.

VOICES: The Power, Pain, & Purpose of Voices

Pickleball is a metaphor for leading organizations today: A lot of things look similar to what we did in the past, but the culture and delivery systems are different. Churches used to connect with people primarily on Sunday mornings, but now most of our people are on social media every day (and often dozens of times a day!). We can reach them with our online voice at all hours wherever we are and wherever they are. Our connections, then, are similar but different. We teach the Bible, but biblical illiteracy is on the rise, so we can't make as many assumptions about people understanding the context of a passage (if they can even find it!). Our voice of teaching and preaching has to change to fit the audience. They used to bring Bibles; now we have passages on the screen. In the past, careers were long and stable. In the church, like the corporate world, people often spend their entire careers with one church or one company. No longer. Today, staff members see themselves as free agents, always open to a better offer.

In every kind of organization, our products and services may look like they did in the past, but today, we're playing pickleball, not tennis, and we need to be aware of all the adjustments so our voice meets people where they are to inspire and challenge them.

In case you're wondering, the audience for this book includes pastors and their staff teams, as well as business leaders and their teams. Some of the points, research, and applications are written for churches, but all of the research and quotes can be applied to a wide, inclusive audience.

THE POWER OF A VOICE

Not long ago, my wife Brenda was talking to our eleven-year-old granddaughter Rose, who had been a cheerleader. Brenda asked her about her plans for the upcoming season. Here's how it went:

Brenda: "Hey, Rose, are you going out for cheerleading next year again?"

Rose, shaking her head: "No!"

Brenda, surprised: "Why not?"

Rose: "Because."

Brenda: "Because...?

Rose, both defiant and disgusted: "Because an older cheerleader made me crazy."

Brenda: "What happened?"

Rose: "She said I jumped around too much, and my skirt didn't fit right."

Brenda, with a voice both strong and kind, said: "Let me tell you the truth. You are a terrific cheerleader, and you're beautiful! Don't let others' voices keep you from doing what you want to do."

VOICES: The Power, Pain, & Purpose of Voices

Brenda, Rose's loving grandma, wanted to make sure that her voice was stronger than the voice of the older cheerleader—and the one Rose would remember.

> "What injects fulfillment, purpose, and joy into my life? What fills my tank so I'm never running on empty?"

Zig Ziglar had a way of capturing what's most important in relationships. He said, "You never know when a moment and a few sincere words can have an impact on a life forever."[2] Words have incredible power to comfort or harm, to build up or destroy, to inspire or shatter. As I meet with leaders from across the world, I've seen that the voices they hear and the voices they speak shape identity, meaning, and value. The question each of us needs to ask isn't, "What should I do now?" but ones that should precede it: "What injects fulfillment, purpose, and joy into my life? What fills my tank so I'm never running on empty?" And when we've answered those questions for ourselves, we'll be ready to ask them of those around us.

As leaders develop through stages of organizational growth—and as they get older and perhaps wiser (or perhaps more fragile from all the bumps and bruises of leading people)—internal and external voices get louder. We need to be more aware of how our words affect the people on our teams and, even more, the people who live under our roofs. But we also need to be objective about the voices that are shaping us.

> As leaders, we're targets . . . it's part of the job description . . . the territory we occupy.

We may want to be seen as impervious to criticism, but only sociopaths can claim that trait! We live for encouragement, and we slowly wilt without it. The voices we hear have the power to inspire us to greatness, sandpaper our confidence to dust, or crush us like a sledgehammer. As leaders, we're targets . . . it's part

VOICES: The Power, Pain, & Purpose of Voices

of the job description... the territory we occupy. This means we need even more encouragement, not less.

What voices occupy space in your mind?

In a *Forbes* magazine article about leaders communicating to staff members and employees, Lori Harris, managing partner at Harris Whitesell Consulting, cites studies showing that the primary reason people fail to communicate well is fear: the fear of others not valuing what they say, which would make them feel "less than." This self-reinforcing fear creates a higher barrier to scale the next time honesty and openness are called for. Excellent communication skills aren't add-ons for leaders; they're essential so we and those we lead overcome our innate fears. The benefits?

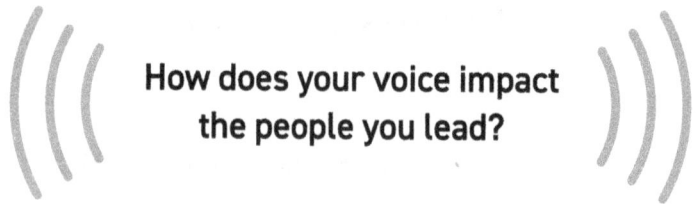

How does your voice impact the people you lead?

Harris lists them:

Moving beyond our communication fears, we open ourselves to discovering and learning key communication competencies and skills necessary to having effective and productive conversations and empowering ourselves with courage, humility and discipline to maximize communication competencies that create better relationships, resulting in higher levels of trust, and communications that align to vision, values and priorities. The organization benefits include clear vision, high-performing teams, an increase in employee engagement and productivity, effective collaboration and innovation and increased profitability. When people remove the distortion, they open themselves up to utilizing key communication tactics and skills, experiencing meaningful and productive conversations.[3]

How does your voice impact the people you lead?

Yes, what we *do* is important. There's no question about that. But what we do, and especially *why* we do it, is a product of *the voices* we've internalized. The quality of our leadership is based on the messages we've heard and still believe. These fill our hearts, and as Jesus said, "For the mouth speaks what the heart is full of" (Luke 6:45).

God has made us relational people, and we've been deeply shaped by the voices we've heard. Some of these have been extraordinarily positive and have breathed

VOICES: The Power, Pain, & Purpose of Voices

life into us, but others have smelled rotten. Some of us are well aware of how the voices we've heard have shaped us, but many are so forward-focused that they don't take time to reflect. Steve Jobs wasn't known for his theological expertise, but in his 2005 commencement address at Stanford, he encouraged graduates to take the time to look at the past. He described a number of colossal failures and detours in his leadership at Apple. At the time each of these occurred, he was frustrated and angry, but later he realized each setback had played an important role in his future success. He told the audience, "You can't connect the dots looking forward; you can only connect them looking backward. So you have to trust that the dots will somehow connect in your future."[4]

Recently, I've become more intensely aware of the voices of people who have shaped me. Let me share a few of them.

Parents

When I was a little boy, my father told me the story of Samuel. His mother, Hannah, was barren. The historian tells us,

In her deep anguish Hannah prayed to the LORD, weeping bitterly. And she made a vow, saying, "LORD Almighty, if you will only look on your

servant's misery and remember me, and not forget your servant but give her a son, then I will give him to the LORD for all the days of his life."
—1 Samuel 1:10-11

Eli, the priest, heard her anguished prayer and thought she was drunk. She assured him she was quite sober but quite heartbroken. Eli told her, "Go in peace, and may the God of Israel grant you what you have asked of him" (1 Samuel 1:17). Hannah went home to her husband Elkanah, and nine months later, a baby was born. "She named him Samuel, saying, 'Because I asked the LORD for him'" (1 Samuel 1:20).

When my father told me this story, he turned to me and said, "We named you Samuel, too, because you are our son of promise!" My mother died in 1982, and my father passed away in 1991, but their powerfully affirming words are rooted deep in my heart.

Friends

When I was struggling to figure out how an Indian man could serve God in America, I had many conflicting thoughts and emotions. Was I insane for trying to become a pastor... of mostly white people? Should I just give up and find a job where no one cared about the color of my skin or my accent?

VOICES: The Power, Pain, & Purpose of Voices

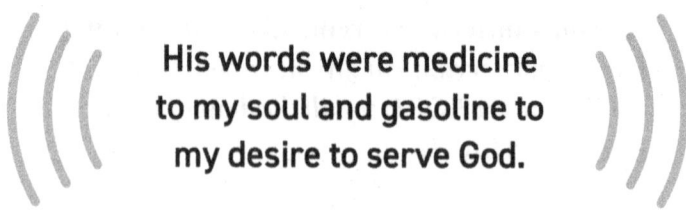

His words were medicine to my soul and gasoline to my desire to serve God.

When I was at my lowest point, my friend Dr. Rich Edwards looked me in the eye and said, "Sam, you will be successful in whatever you do." His words were medicine to my soul and gasoline to my desire to serve God.

Teachers

When I was a freshman in college, I was the only foreigner in my class. My teacher, Miss Smith, kept her gaze on me day after day. I'm not sure what stories she'd heard about students from my homeland, but one day she asked me to move to the front row. She accused me of cheating, and she wanted to have me closer so she could watch me more closely. I vividly remember that moment and the shame of being falsely accused in front of the entire class.

Strangers

On my very first full day in America, in August of 1973, I woke up early in the men's dormitory at Beulah

Voices We've Heard

Heights Bible College, got dressed, and walked outside. It had been dark the night before when I arrived, and I wanted to see the campus in the morning light. As I walked around, I came up to a little girl about four or five years old. She was going to be the first person I met, and I was excited to connect with someone. I stopped, bent down, and smiled. I said, "Hello! How are you this morning? My name is Sam. I'm from India."

She stared at me for a few seconds, scrunched up her face, and said, "You're weird!" And she walked off.

Even though I knew it was only the instant reaction of a little kid and a stranger's voice, her words were powerful—like a dull knife stabbed into my heart. My very first encounter in a new land was the voice of rejection, and it stayed with me for a long time. (That's obvious, because I still vividly remember it fifty-plus years later!) To be honest, she was right. To her, I'm sure I looked and sounded weird. I was a scrawny young man of about 125 pounds, and if you think my accent is pronounced now, you wouldn't have understood a word I said back then.

I meet many people at churches and conferences. I try to connect with them, looking them in the eye and listening carefully when they tell me a bit about themselves. Almost always, people respond with genuine appreciation. They appreciate being known.

VOICES: The Power, Pain, & Purpose of Voices

MY FIRST BOARD MEETING

When we lead our first board meeting—either in our first pastorate or when we're new to an organization—we want to start strong. We expect things to go well. After all, they hired us, didn't they? But sometimes, we can be blindsided. I told this story in my book, *How Leaders Create Chaos and Why They Should*:

In July of 1980, my wife Brenda and I moved to Hartford, Michigan, where I accepted the call to be the Pastor of a small, rural church. Actually, the church was more than three miles from the little town. The closest blinking light was more than two miles from the church. The nearest McDonald's was eighteen miles away. When I stepped through the door for the first time, I was a lion. I saw myself as a change agent, someone who would lead men and women to do magnificent things for God and transform their community. My daydreams painted vivid pictures of remarkable growth in our church and rich discipleship among our people. We would be known as a congregation that eagerly fulfilled the Great Commandment and the Great Commission, and I had a lot of ideas about what we could do. Before my first Board meeting just days after we moved into the parsonage, which shared a wall with the church, I looked at church listings *in the local Yellow Pages. (Remember those? If you're under forty, probably not.) I saw that it was possible for us to put our church's name and information in a box so it would stand out from the rest. When I called the phone company, I was told the additional charge would be only $5 a month. In the Board meeting that first week, I made the recommendation to spend this very modest sum, but the men in the room flatly turned me down. In that moment, a thousand thoughts sped through my mind. If they wouldn't respect my leadership enough to spend $5 a month to give our church a little more recognition, what did it mean for my future there? It was obvious that they didn't see me as an inspiring, effective leader; I was just the hired "main event" on Sunday mornings, Sunday nights, Sunday school, and Wednesday nights—that's four different messages every week. But that's not all. A couple of families in the church could have stepped out of a movie about the feud between the Hatfields and McCoys. They were fierce and always ready for a fight. They'd run off previous pastors, and they were proud of their place of power in the church ... and now they had their sights set on me. I had walked into a room full of explosives, and I was carrying a lit match!*[5]

VOICES: The Power, Pain, & Purpose of Voices

THE VOICE

God speaks. He spoke, and the universe came into existence. He spoke to Noah and rescued a remnant from the flood. He spoke to Abraham and promised to bless him so he could pay it forward and be a blessing to all nations. He spoke to Moses, Joshua, David, the prophets, and anyone else who would listen.

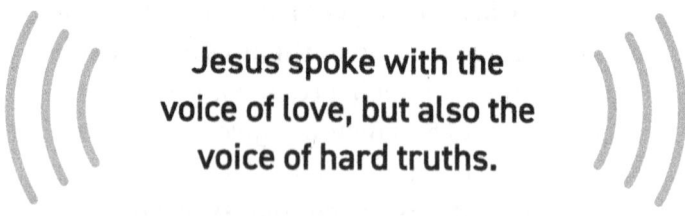

Jesus spoke with the voice of love, but also the voice of hard truths.

And then he spoke through his Son.

Jesus spoke with the voice of love, but also the voice of hard truths. John's Gospel contains more sharp disagreements between Jesus and the religious leaders than the Synoptic Gospels. In chapter after chapter, we see Jesus wading into conflict with them. His purpose was to turn their hearts toward God and, too, to assure those who were watching and listening (like all believers who have read John's account, including you and me) that his message wasn't like the Pharisees and Sadducees. In one of

Voices We've Heard

His most famous scenes, He contrasts himself as "the gatekeeper" of God's sheep with "strangers," who were "thieves and robbers" who come "to steal and kill and destroy." But how does "the Good Shepherd" protect and guide his sheep? By his voice. Jesus told the rigid, self-righteous Pharisees:

*The gatekeeper opens the gate for him, and the sheep listen to his **voice**. He calls his own sheep by name and leads them out. When he has brought out all his own, he goes on ahead of them, and his sheep follow him because they know his voice. But they will never follow a stranger; in fact, they will run away from him because they do not recognize a stranger's voice." Jesus used this figure of speech, but the Pharisees did not understand what he was telling them.—John 10:3-6 (author emphasis added)*

Jesus' sheep "listen to his voice," "know his voice," and don't recognize "a stranger's voice"—in other words, a stranger's voice sounds "off," it doesn't ring true, and it's self-serving and manipulative. The voice of Jesus changed confused, self-absorbed men into people who would "turn the world upside down." They didn't just have a written job description; they had

VOICES: The Power, Pain, & Purpose of Voices

Him, and through the Spirit, they kept listening to His voice as they followed his leading.

You and I have heard many voices over the years. It's my contention that many of them have inspired us, but too often, we've listened to voices that have shaken our confidence and burdened us with doubts. Our first step, then, is to be more perceptive about the voices we've heard—the affirming, the inspiring, the harshly critical, and the blaming—so we have a clear choice about the voices we allow to shape our lives today.

Michelle Woods Waldron penned a poem called "Voices":

> *Voices can be loud*
> *Voices can be soft*
> *Voices can giggle and laugh*
> *Voices can sing like a lark*
> *Voices can whisper*
> *Or shout oh so loud*
> *Voices are powerful*
> *Speak well*
> *Use your voice wisely.*[6]

Whose voice is resident in your head?

Voices We've Heard

At the end of each chapter, you'll find some questions to stimulate reflection. You may want to use these with your team and, perhaps, your family.

THINK ABOUT IT:
1) What are some of the most affirming voices you've heard throughout your life?

2) Take yourself back there. What did you feel when those words were spoken? What difference did these people make when they spoke to you this way?

3) As you read this chapter, you've probably had a flashback or two of harsh, uncaring things people have said to you. What were the messages, both verbal and non-verbal? What did you feel when you heard these messages? What impact did they have on you—short-term and long-term?

4) What are some of the strangest and funniest things people have said to you?

VOICES: The Power, Pain, & Purpose of Voices

> THE VOICE IN YOUR
> HEAD BECOMES THE
> VOICE IN YOUR MOUTH.
> THE VOICE IN YOUR MOUTH
> BECOMES THE VOICE
> IN OTHERS' HEADS.

CHAPTER 2

Voices We've Ignored

IT WAS MONDAY NIGHT, AND PASTOR ROBERT'S WIFE, Karen, became concerned. That morning, he had read an email from one of the people who had heard him preach the day before, and it really upset him. When he walked into the house, she could tell something was wrong. His clenched teeth, his furrowed brow, and his head tilted down... she asked, "What's wrong, Hon?"

"Nothing," he almost snarled.

Karen put her hands on her hips, smiled, and told him, "Yeah, right. Nothing." She paused for a second

VOICES: The Power, Pain, & Purpose of Voices

and asked again, "Did you find out a meteor is headed for Earth, and we're all doomed?"

Robert chuckled, "No, it's worse than that. I got a note from Sarah Martin. She thought my sermon yesterday stank."

Karen tilted her head and asked, "Is that the word she used?"

"No, but she might as well have used it."

> **Many leaders are subconsciously far too open to voices that condemn, berate, and discourage them.**

Karen knew that Sarah Martin's criticism wasn't really the problem. Robert, like all leaders, gets all kinds of feedback—some encouraging, some not so much; some helpful, and some off the mark. She rattled off a series of questions, not waiting for him to answer: "Again? You're going to let one negative remark color your perception? Do you remember all the people who were so highly complementary as they walked out and shook your hand yesterday? What about them? Do you value their feedback as much as Sarah's?"

Robert had embraced one negative voice and ignored scores of positive voices. Many of us are just like him—we use a filter to let some voices in and keep others out, but we use the wrong filter.

VOICES WE FILTER IN . . . BUT SHOULDN'T

Certainly, we need to be open to criticism, but many leaders are subconsciously *far too open* to voices that condemn, berate, and discourage them. Psychologist Pete Walker coined the term "inner critic," which he describes as internal messages triggered by thoughts of past failures and hurt, a thought process that "weds shame and self-hate about imperfection to fear of abandonment, and mercilessly drive the psyche with entwined serpents of perfectionism and endangerment."[7]

We'll address the inner critic and toxic messages in more detail later, but for now, it's helpful to at least touch on some of the negative voices in our heads. Does Walker's description of the inner critic sound overblown and extreme for what most of us experience? Maybe . . . maybe not. Do our failures haunt us? Does fear lurk underneath our demonstrations of strength

VOICES: The Power, Pain, & Purpose of Voices

and confidence? I'm not saying that we all wrestle with a fierce, harsh, inner critic, but many of us do.

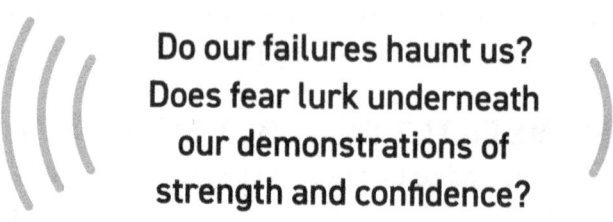

> Do our failures haunt us? Does fear lurk underneath our demonstrations of strength and confidence?

Voices of Shame

Professor Brené Brown has written and spoken extensively about the causes and impact of shame. She defines it this way: "Shame is the feeling you get when you believe that you're not worthy of anyone caring about you or loving you. That you're such a bad person that you can't even blame other people for not caring about you. You just want the floor to swallow you up."[8] She insists the belief that we're "less than" is common to all of us, at least to some extent. Our experience of shame can crush our spirits, but it awakens our capacity for empathy for others who are struggling. But shame, by its nature, thrives in the dark where the light of love and grace doesn't shine. Brown explains why we try to keep it hidden, as well as why it's so important to be honest about it with at least one person:

Shame derives its power from being unspeakable. That's why it loves perfectionists—it's so easy to keep us quiet. If we cultivate enough awareness about shame to name it and speak to it, we've basically cut it off at the knees. Shame hates having words wrapped around it. If we speak shame, it begins to wither. Just the way exposure to light was deadly for the gremlins, language and story bring light to shame and destroy it."[9]

> **Superiority shows up most often by putting others down.**

Voices of Inferiority

Another common faulty filter is trying to overcome our inferiority by insisting on our superiority. In other words, we over-compensate for our sense of being flawed and vulnerable by telling ourselves (and anyone who will listen) that we're the smartest, wisest,

VOICES: The Power, Pain, & Purpose of Voices

best-looking, and overall coolest cat on the street! We project that we have it all together.

When those in our families or on our teams realize "the emperor has no clothes," trust is eroded, and people spend their time jockeying for position—playing it safe by not speaking up and creating alliances to cope with the stress. Superiority shows up most often by putting others down. I know a leader who always finds fault with everyone and everything they try to do. By putting them down, he thinks he's elevating himself. That's his illusion. A few on the outside may buy his bravado, but those who live and work with him see through the charade. He's hurting himself far more than he's hurting those he criticizes.

Those are just a few of the voices we filter in ... but shouldn't.

VOICES WE FILTER OUT ... BUT SHOULDN'T

I make a choice to listen to this podcast or that one, this sermon or that one, this news program or that one. I make choices all day to filter what comes into my mind. Many of us need to do a better job of choosing the voices we listen to.

Like Pastor Robert, many of us—no matter our calling and vocation—let caustic messages sink deep into our hearts, and we ignore those that are affirming and bring life. Too often, we ignore...

People who believe in us.

I'm not sure what was more meaningful to me: my father's story and pronouncement that I was their "son of promise," or the confident and thrilled look on his face. My parents are gone now, but there has been another person who has believed in me since 1979: my wife Brenda. When I wonder if I'm making a difference, or when I listen to my inner critic and enough outer critics, she is the rock I can stand on. Why in the world would I ignore her voice? Why would I discount the conclusions of the person who knows me best and receive harsh messages from those who don't know me, haven't heard my story, and probably don't want to know what's behind what I say and do?

> **Many of us let caustic messages sink deep into our hearts, and we ignore those that are affirming and bring life.**

VOICES: The Power, Pain, & Purpose of Voices

People who try to warn us.

Solomon noted, "Wounds from a friend can be trusted, but an enemy multiplies kisses" (Proverbs 27:6). We often ignore words from even our closest friends if they make us feel uncomfortable. Leaders got into their roles because they exhibited a high level of talent and confidence, and some of us read our glowing bios a little too often! Those who really care about us wade in and tell us things we may not want to hear. They hold up a mirror so we can see ourselves more clearly. They may talk about our drive and neglect of our families, how we treat people on our teams, our chronic exhaustion, our counseling with the person getting a divorce, or a hundred other potential (or very real) problems that can trip us up.

We ignore their warnings for any of several reasons:

1) We didn't ask them for their input.

If we don't ask, we assume they have no right to speak up. Maybe they initiated because they've warned us before and we didn't listen, or they see us getting too close to the edge, or we insist, "Hey, I'm fine. Don't worry about it."

2) They don't have the right.
We may have a pecking order of who we let speak into our lives, and that staff member, board member, or family member isn't at the level that warrants our attention. (Why, then, do we accept the critiques of people in our congregations we hardly know?)

> **Confidence is a valuable leadership trait if it's coupled with humility, but it's deadly when arrogance blinds us.**

3) They whisper too softly.
Many people are hesitant to speak up and warn us of a danger they see in our leadership. A few may resemble a fire alarm, but most are so timid that they don't deliver the message with enough strength to make a dent.

4) We're sure we know better.
We hear the warning, but we insist that we've already thought it through, weighed the upsides and

VOICES: The Power, Pain, & Purpose of Voices

downsides, and told the person, "I'm good. There's nothing to see here." Confidence is a valuable leadership trait if it's coupled with humility, but it's deadly when arrogance blinds us.

5) The time ... or the place ... or the method isn't right.

We can be pretty creative in coming up with excuses for ignoring a warning! Maybe we've had practice before this moment or maybe we thought of an excuse on the fly. Either way, we brush the person off so we don't have to listen. "Maybe some other time," we promise ... or almost promise.

6) If they've been wrong before ...

If someone has tried to wave a yellow flag in the past but their warning proved to be needless, it's easy to blow them off the next time.

> They leave with confidence we've heard and we'll take action; we smile but forget the conversation within minutes.

7) We act like we're listening, but we're really not.
Some of us are so smooth. We've mastered the talent of appearing to be engaged in a conversation when we checked out after the first few words. When people find the courage to speak up to us, we make eye contact and lean forward, but we have no intention of processing what they're warning us about. When they leave the room, we thank them for their candor. They leave with confidence we've heard and we'll take action; we smile but forget the conversation within minutes.

People who affirm our role.
The inner critic can drown out the affirming, validating voices of those who identify our talents, gifting, and role as leaders. In one way or another, sometimes using this terminology and sometimes not, they say that our impact follows one of Christ's roles as prophet, priest, and king. For instance, those who function primarily in prophetic gifts are talented teachers, those who have priestly gifts are empathetic and compassionate, and those whose contribution to the church is kingly are skilled at organization and administration. (We can identify these three primary roles in the leaders of nonprofits and businesses, too.) Of course,

VOICES: The Power, Pain, & Purpose of Voices

all of us need at least a modicum of abilities in each area, but we may excel in one of them.

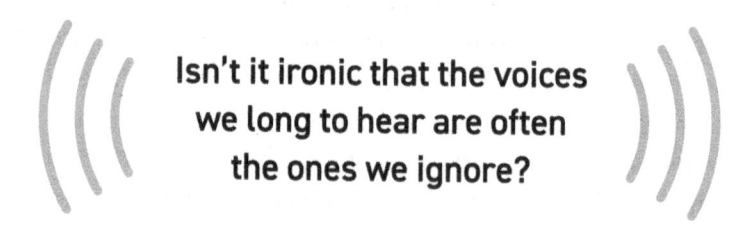

> **Isn't it ironic that the voices we long to hear are often the ones we ignore?**

Why would we ignore those who see these abilities at work in and through us? Because our inferiority is like stuffing our ears with cotton so we can't hear it, but then taking the cotton out when anyone says anything critical of us.

Isn't it ironic that the voices we long to hear are often the ones we ignore? Yes, we need a filter to determine what comes through the noise to penetrate our hearts, but we need the right filter. A friend told me he cut his grass early one spring when oak tassels covered the ground. When he went out to cut the grass the next week, his mower wouldn't start. He checked the oil, the gas, and the pull. They all seemed fine. Then he had an idea to take off the air filter to see if it was clean. It was completely clogged. He knocked it a few times against a tree to dislodge all the gunk and put it back in. He pulled the cord, and the mower cranked right up.

My friend didn't have the wrong filter, but he had an ineffective one. It was so packed with gunk that his perfectly good mower wouldn't work. For him, it was a simple fix. As a metaphor for us, we learn an important concept: whether we have the wrong filter or a clogged filter, we need to take action to be sure we have one that works. Far too often, we let caustic voices speak to our hearts, and we ignore those we desperately need to hear.

THINK ABOUT IT:

1) Can you relate to Pastor Robert in the opening story of this chapter? If so, how?

2) What are some voices you allow to be too loud and too frequent?

3) What are some important voices you've ignored?

4) Describe what it will take to replace your filter.

VOICES: The Power, Pain, & Purpose of Voices

THE VOICE IN YOUR HEAD
BECOMES THE VOICE
IN YOUR MOUTH.
THE VOICE IN YOUR MOUTH
BECOMES THE VOICE
IN OTHERS' HEADS.

CHAPTER 3

Voices of Toxic Messages

PASTOR BRAD SEEMED LIKE A VERY HAPPY GUY. HE meets people easily and is attentive in conversations. I met him years ago, and we saw each other at events over the course of a decade or so. At a recent conference, he asked if we could meet. "I want to talk to you about some things," he said obliquely.

"Sure," I responded. "How about lunch tomorrow?"

When we met at the restaurant, he asked the waiter to take us to a table far in the back. I thought this was a bit odd. Maybe he didn't want to be in the main room

VOICES: The Power, Pain, & Purpose of Voices

where it was too loud. When we sat down, a waiter brought us menus and water. Brad didn't even glance at the menu. He took a big drink of water and almost whispered, "Sam, I don't think I can take it anymore."

"What do you mean?"

"I've tried really hard to be a good pastor, a good leader for my team, and a good friend to many in our church, but I'm exhausted...burned out."

I was surprised. Only minutes earlier, he was talking with people outside the restaurant, shaking hands, smiling, asking about their families, and looking like a picture of security and happiness. "Tell me what's going on," I invited him.

He took a deep breath and began to tell me much more of his story than I'd ever heard before, and I was sure, much more than he'd shared with anyone else, maybe including his wife. He described growing up in a home where his parents fought a lot, sometimes physically and always cruelly. "I was the designated peacemaker," he explained. "I was only a kid, but I took the role of trying to reduce the tension between my mom and dad."

"That's a lot of pressure," I interjected.

"Yeah, and when they got a divorce, I thought it was on me."

"On you?" I asked, looking for more.

Voices of Toxic Messages

"I felt like a failure...a colossal failure." He paused for a few seconds and then told me, "Actually, I still do. It colors everything I am and everything I do." He paused again, and with his eyes filling with tears, he asked, "Sam, can you help me?"

When Brad asked to speak with me the day before, I assumed he wanted advice about leading his team or growing his church. We were talking about something far more important: his heart, his haunted past, and his future as a husband, father, and pastor.

> **The problem is that we give toxic messages far too much space in our heads.**

Like many of us, Pastor Brad had internalized toxic messages from his past. In the deepest recesses of his heart, he believed he was a failure. He had spent the decades since the divorce becoming skilled in image management—trying to look calm and confident on the outside while he felt weak and ashamed on the inside.

VOICES: The Power, Pain, & Purpose of Voices

Sometimes, they're loud and fierce, and sometimes, they're no more than whispers. The problem is that we give toxic messages far too much space in our heads.

It's important—crucial, really—to identify the toxic messages as, well... toxic. Too often and too long, we've lived with them, and they feel normal and right. They aren't. They're "flaming arrows of the evil one" (Ephesians 6:16), meant to destroy us. Paul encourages us to bring evil into the light: "But everything exposed by the light becomes visible—and everything that is illuminated becomes a light" (Ephesians 5:13).

> **Toxic voices create wounds, but the light of God's truth and grace brings healing.**

Light has a restorative nature. The National Institutes of Health and NASA have found that red and infrared wavelengths of light are absorbed by an important enzyme in cellular metabolism, accelerating the healing of wounds, reducing levels of pain, and preventing the loss of eyesight in some cases. A NASA report explains:

> *Through experimentation, the researchers showed that high-intensity red and near-infrared LEDs significantly accelerated the healing of oxygen-deprived wounds in rats and also sped the growth and proliferation of skin, bone, and muscle cell cultures from mice and rats. The team supplied LED devices to U.S. Navy crews for treatment of training injuries. These produced more than a 40 percent greater improvement in musculoskeletal injuries and a 50 percent faster healing time for lacerations, compared to control groups.[10]*

Toxic voices create wounds, but the light of God's truth and grace brings healing. Let's expose those messages and call them what they are: evil and destructive.

THE INNER CRITIC REVISITED

In the last chapter, we identified our negative self-talk as "the inner critic." Now, let's look more closely at some of the language that, for many of us, sounds so familiar. We've internalized caustic messages so now we use our own voices to tell ourselves:

"I'm such a fool."

"I can't afford to fail, or else..."

VOICES: The Power, Pain, & Purpose of Voices

"I can't do anything right."
"What if people really knew me?"
"I can't let my guard down."
"I don't deserve to be happy."
"There's no use in even trying."
"I'm worthless, hopeless, helpless."
"I'm such a loser."

Amazingly, some of the most accomplished people actually believe things like this. They spend their lives desperately trying to prove their inner critic wrong.

"No One Understands."

Like Pastor Brad, a lot of leaders are on the edge of giving up. A series of surveys revealed an alarming trend: In the span of only a few years, the number of pastors who considered quitting rose from 29 percent to 42 percent and then to 53 percent. Certainly, the stress caused by recent global events was a major factor, but the stress hasn't gone away. Scott Thumma, professor of Sociology of Religion at Hartford International University and director of the Hartford Institute for Religion Research observes,

> *The further we are from the onset of the COVID-19 pandemic, the more we observe larger percentages of clergy pondering alternatives to their present congregation, vocation, or both....*

Voices of Toxic Messages

While there is some overlap in these two thoughts, it is not entirely the same group of leaders considering leaving both their current congregation and the ministry profession altogether. About a third of leaders report having both thoughts, a third have considered one or the other (11% consider only leaving their congregation and 20% consider only leaving the profession) and the final third have never considered leaving either.[11]

For leaders in any organization on the cusp of burnout (and those who are already past the red line), the messages can sound like:

"I'm exhausted."

"Nobody understands all the stress I'm under."

"Nobody appreciates how hard I work."

"I do all I can do, and it's never enough."

"It's over. I've had it. It's just too much. I need to get a job as a greeter at The Home Depot."

We've played the comparison and competition game, and we've concluded that we've lost ... for good ... and we'll never be able to come back.

But some leaders use the belief that no one will understand as cover for major mess ups. They've developed a counseling or reporting relationship that's become too intimate, too familiar, too close to

VOICES: The Power, Pain, & Purpose of Voices

the line... and actually over the line. Or they've fudged the accounts so they can draw more money to cover family debts. They watch porn, they've gotten into online sports gambling, they've said or done horrible things at home—the list is endless. They live in fear of being found out, and they've tried to convince themselves, "No one will ever know," "It's not a big deal," "No one appreciates all the stress I'm under. I need a break," and "Other people have done far worse." But they can't get the nagging sense of guilt and fear out of their minds. The voice that says, "No one understands me," tries to drown out the Spirit's conviction, but the voice is strong.

> They live in fear of being found out, and they've tried to convince themselves, "No one will ever know."

"Everything Feels Out of Control."
For many of us, the pandemic shook our sense of safety and security—not just from the fear of

contracting the disease, but the shutdowns forced us to radically change our strategy and expectations. Rita McGrath, author of *Transient Advantage*, asserts that the insecurity in leadership is still affected by COVID-19:

It's going to be a while before we truly make sense of 2023. A pervasive sense of uncertainty seemed to linger in the atmosphere. New projects got put on hold, once-exuberant tech companies laid people off, and we're still suffering the lingering after-effects of the pandemic in ways large and small.

She draws a number of conclusions that are consistent with leaders who feel like the ground has shifted under their feet:

- » We used to assume stability was normal, but now we realize change is the new normal.
- » We need to use our best resources to take advantage of our best opportunities.
- » Innovation is a requirement, not a sideshow.
- » We need to find and promote leaders who are "discovery-driven, create psychological safety, and get information directly from the 'edges.'"
- » We need to realize that many of our team members see their current work as a "tour of duty"

VOICES: The Power, Pain, & Purpose of Voices

and don't expect to spend their careers with one organization.

McGrath doesn't try to move culture back to pre-pandemic mode. Instead, change has become a way of life, but it doesn't need to be an existential threat:

When you practice the principles of transient advantage effectively, you can create a pipeline of new advantages that allow you to catch the 'waves' of opportunity as they gather, crest, and fall away. I believe it's how we will compete in the future. Or at least how the winners will compete in the future![12]

The culture is roaring forward on the wings of innovation, a fact that makes many of us feel left behind and out of control.

> We've played the comparison and competition game, and we're winning!

Voices of Toxic Messages

"Look at Me!"

For some of us, the messages sound very different. We're not crushed by past failures and the fear of the future. We're riding high on a wave of success. We've played the comparison and competition game, and we're winning! Our emotions are a blend of relief, gratitude, and superiority. It feels good... really good, but after a week or a month of relative euphoria, we look up the ladder and see the pastor of a church that's bigger than ours, and pride returns to the very real fear of not measuring up.

> **God calls us to give our all every day and leave the results to him.**

In an article titled "Six Toxic Thoughts Successful People Quarantine," Dr. Travis Bradberry warns leaders who are doing well about inner voices that can crater them and their careers. The six, with my commentary, include:

VOICES: The Power, Pain, & Purpose of Voices

» Toxic Voice #1: Perfection equals success.

Driven people strive to be the very best, and they can't stand even small and momentary setbacks. In other words, they give far too much credibility to their inner voices that tell them, "You can't afford to mess this up ... even a little!"

» Toxic Voice #2: Destiny is predetermined.

Yes, we believe in God's sovereignty, and our gracious God may give us stunning success. But we need to remember that many (if not all) of the greatest leaders in the Bible suffered long periods of failure, opposition, and heaven's silence. God calls us to give our all every day and leave the results to him.

» Toxic Voice #3: I "always" or "never" do that.

When we use these all-encompassing inclusive and exclusive words, we're fooling ourselves that we're in complete control of ourselves and our situations, and we set ourselves up for deep disappointment.

» Toxic Voice #4: I'm a success because others see me as a success.

Over the years, I've noticed that the public (including the people in our churches) often have a view of us that's far too positive or far too negative.

Voices of Toxic Messages

If our sense of calling and self-worth is based on their opinions, we're on very shaky ground.

» Toxic Voice #5: My past equals my future.

It doesn't. God's plan is beyond human comprehension. Moses' past as a murderer and vagabond didn't predict his future as the one God called to lead the people out of Egypt. And Elijah's past as the one God chose to miraculously defeat the prophets of Baal didn't predict his future terror of Jezebel and his deep depression. We can and should learn from our past, but God is far too creative to be tied to it.

» Toxic Voice #6: My emotions equal reality.

They don't. When we refuse to look at hard realities, our emotions might be very positive, but it's an illusion. Or when our feelings are based on "what ifs" and "if onlys," we can be discouraged even in the midst of success and growth.

Bradberry asserts that to be successful leaders, we need to "quarantine" these misguided voices.[13] To quarantine means to identify and isolate them. That's an important (and sometimes difficult) step, but it's not all. We also need to replace them with positive messages. (We'll get to that later.)

VOICES: The Power, Pain, & Purpose of Voices

"Not Yet. Maybe Then."

Psychology Today conducted a survey asking 52,000 Americans the open-ended question, "What does it take to make you happy?" The answers were varied, but many responded that their happiness is contingent on particular circumstances: "When" this happens, "then" I'll be happy. We sometimes hear people say, "If I could just win the lottery!" So the contingency is a lot of money. But how much is enough? What if the jackpot is higher for the next winner? "Darn, I should have waited!"

With more disposable income comes conspicuous consumption. "I'd like a Bentley or a Lamborghini. Or I'll build a new house ... with a swimming pool and tennis court. Then I'll be happy!"

Others have relational "when-then" models. "When I find the right person, then I'll get married and be happy." But about half of those who believed that promise at some point conclude, "When I get a divorce, then I'll be happy!" Or "When I have children..." "When they're out of diapers..." "When the teenagers leave home..."

Church leaders may assume this superficiality doesn't apply to them, but does it? How about, "When our church grows to 300 (or 500 or 1,000 or 2,000 or whatever benchmark is next), then I'll be happy."

Voices of Toxic Messages

"When I have a great staff team (and not some of the people with me now)..." "When the rich people in town start coming to our church—and they tithe..." "When I get invited to speak at the next big conference..." And business leaders drive themselves to exhaustion to reach the next level of growth. They think, *When I get there, I can slow down and relax*, but even as they approach a goal, they realize it's not enough. The rat race never ends.

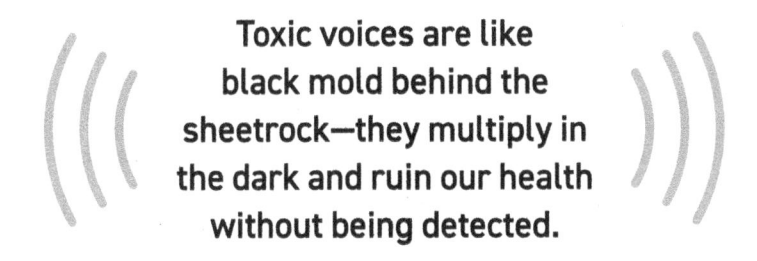

> **Toxic voices are like black mold behind the sheetrock—they multiply in the dark and ruin our health without being detected.**

"When-then" thinking is so common that we don't realize how it robs us of joy today.

Toxic voices are like black mold behind the sheetrock—they multiply in the dark and ruin our health without being detected. They must be brought into the light to be examined and healed. Replacing those voices is hard work. It takes tenacity, wisdom, and

VOICES: The Power, Pain, & Purpose of Voices

encouragement, but it can't happen unless we first identify them clearly.

THINK ABOUT IT:

1) What's the language of your inner critic (we all have one)? Why do these messages seem so right and normal?

2) How does feeling misunderstood affect you? What's your go-to remedy (helpful or unhelpful)?

3) Do you agree or disagree that change has become the new normal, which makes many of us feel out of control?

4) When are comparison and competition healthy? When are they toxic?

5) What are some consequences of "when-then" thinking?

6) Of these forms of toxic messages, which one (or ones) gives you the most trouble? Why?

Voices of Toxic Messages

THE VOICE IN YOUR HEAD BECOMES THE VOICE IN YOUR MOUTH. THE VOICE IN YOUR MOUTH BECOMES THE VOICE IN OTHERS' HEADS.

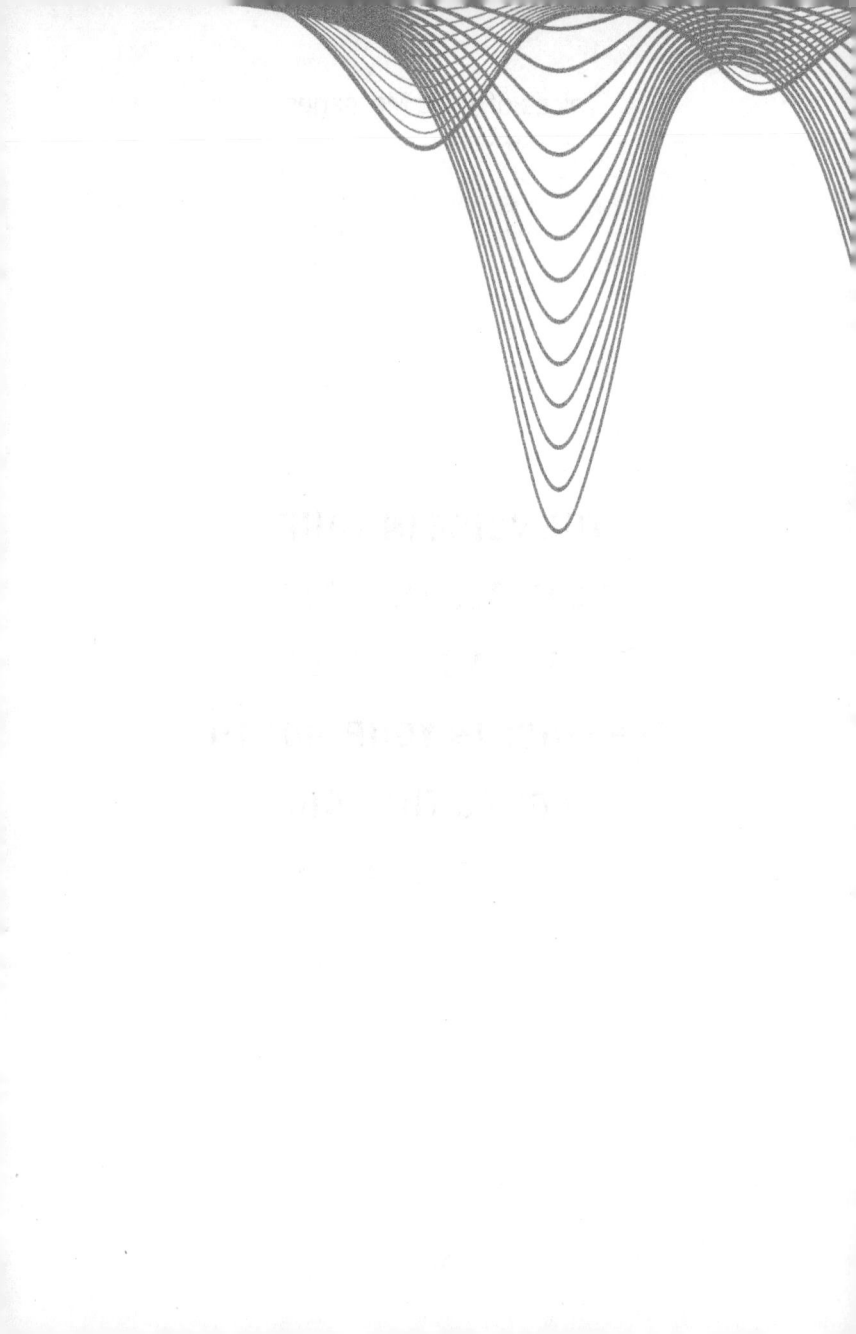

CHAPTER 4

Voices We Long to Hear

FOR DECADES, OPRAH WINFREY HAS BEEN THE QUEEN of talk shows. Millions watch as she interviews comedians and presidents, heroes and criminals. A few years ago, she was interviewed for a program, "Released," on Oprah Winfrey Network, which follows the experiences of former inmates in the months after release from prison. When she was asked about her interviews over the years, she commented, "Everybody that I ever interviewed, after the interview at some point, would say, 'How was that? Was that okay? How'd I do?' And

VOICES: The Power, Pain, & Purpose of Voices

whether it was Barack Obama or Beyoncé or the guy who murdered his kids or the guy who molested kids or someone who had gone on and lost their family. It's incredible that every interviewee—over 4,589 shows and over 37,000 people [I interviewed] one-on-one in person" asked if they did okay. This question, she concluded, is the "common denominator" for all her guests, no matter their background, experience, or position. She reflected, "Everyone just wants to know that you heard me, you saw me, and that what I said mattered."

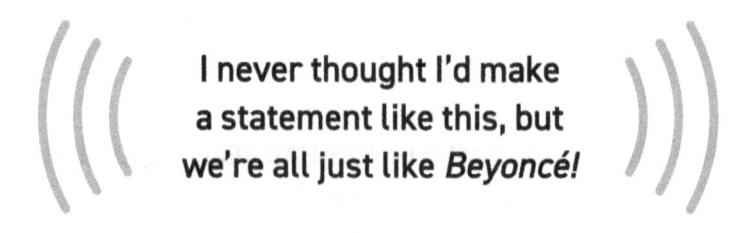

> I never thought I'd make a statement like this, but we're all just like *Beyoncé!*

Winfrey isn't surprised when people who have never been in front of a camera ask this question, but she was stunned at least once. She had Beyoncé on her show, and when the interview concluded, Beyoncé asked if she had done okay. Winfrey looked at her and said, "Girrrrrrrl, you're Beyoncé!"[14]

Voices We Long to Hear

I never thought I'd make a statement like this, but we're all just like Beyoncé! No matter how much success we've enjoyed, no matter how many difficulties we've overcome, we still need to hear voices that validate our value.

> **Anger is a secondary emotion, most often, a reaction to a deeper sense of fear and hurt.**

Encouragement and validation are siblings. Encouragement is giving someone confidence; validation makes a person feel understood and accepted, even if we disagree with one another. A thousand people may encourage us for our leadership skills, and we appreciate it, but it's more meaningful if a handful of people—even one—sees deep into our souls and affirms us without judgment. I've heard grace explained, "God knows the very worst about us and loves us still." That's the voice we need to hear from God, and it's the voice we need to hear from ... someone, anyone!

VOICES: The Power, Pain, & Purpose of Voices

WHEN WE'RE ANGRY

Anger is a secondary emotion, most often, a reaction to a deeper sense of fear and hurt. We want to strike back, we want justice, we want the person to pay for what they've done—whether it's something relatively minor like a child forgetting to close the door or something major like the betrayal of a friend. Anger is a reaction to a threat, but it can feel threatening to all those within the blast radius.

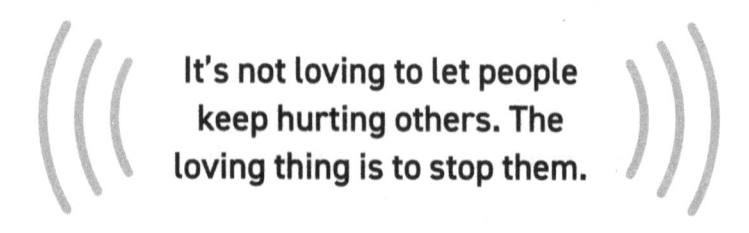

> It's not loving to let people keep hurting others. The loving thing is to stop them.

People around us usually feel uncomfortable when we're angry, and they want us to cool off and calm down so they feel safer. If our anger is "over the top," we certainly do need to calm down, but it doesn't help if the only voice we hear is, "Don't be angry," when we have good reason to be. In the letter to the Ephesians, Paul directed them, "'In your anger do not sin': Do not let the sun go down while you are still angry, and do not give the devil a foothold" (Ephesians 4:26-27).

So, there's sinful anger and righteous anger. Anger at injustice not only isn't sin, it's actually sinful to *not* be angry when it's warranted. John Chrysostom, an early church father, commented,

> *He who does not get angry, when there is just cause for being so, commits sin. For unreasonable patience [that is, refusing to be angry when it's appropriate] is the hotbed of many vices; it fosters negligence and incites not only the wicked but the good to do wrong.*[15]

So, when you have reason to be angry, channel the energy into righting wrongs, caring for the oppressed, protecting the vulnerable, and standing up to bullies for their sake—not to get revenge. It's not loving to let people keep hurting others. The loving thing is to stop them.

Of course, people have a range of reactions to fear and hurt, from explosive rage to passive-aggression to stuffing all the emotions and acting like nothing happened. "Nice Christians," and especially "nice Christian leaders" try to avoid looking like Mt. St. Helen's at the moment the top blew off the volcano, so we often use more subtle techniques of putting

VOICES: The Power, Pain, & Purpose of Voices

people down with sarcasm and claiming, "Hey, it was a joke," or when we're hurt, insisting, "It's no big deal. It didn't bother me at all." Meanwhile, the pressure in the magma chamber builds.

> **Fear is often parallel to hurt: we're afraid of being hurt again, afraid of people who trigger our reactions, and afraid that no one will understand.**

The voice of validation says, "Tell me more about what you're thinking and feeling." This voice isn't threatened by our anger. Instead, we're invited to be open and honest about our perceptions. The voice then asks, "What do you think is under the anger? Could there be some fear or unresolved hurt?" Quite often, the conversation itself validates us. We don't feel condemned, we're not being manipulated to make the person feel better, and the person isn't running away. We can take a deep breath and say, "No, I'm not okay. Thanks for talking to me about how I'm feeling."

WHEN WE'RE HURT OR AFRAID

We want to appear strong, like we have it all together. Many of us feel much more comfortable with our anger than with pain and fear. Anger makes us feel strong; the others make us feel vulnerable. We need someone who will listen, ask open questions, and not give us simplistic solutions to deep and complex problems. Hurts from decades before may have gone unresolved, so they continue to fester. Sooner or later, they resurface and cause problems. Fear is often parallel to hurt: we're afraid of being hurt again, afraid of people who trigger our reactions, and afraid that no one will understand.

We need someone to validate our perceptions and feelings, not "fix" us so we stop feeling that way. People want to help, and they want to be seen as competent but attempts to fix us by rescuing us from our pain don't really help.

When our emotions are validated and accepted, we feel understood, and we can breathe again. Validation makes it easier to turn down the volume of shame that we can't handle life very well. With support and stability, we can then address the nagging fear, self-doubt, and wounds that have haunted our minds for years. We need someone who says something like this:

"I'm sorry that happened to you."

VOICES: The Power, Pain, & Purpose of Voices

"You were really hurt by that."

"I understand why you feel this way. I would too."

"Tell me more about what happened and how you felt."

"Do you want any advice, or do you just want me to listen?"

"What can I do to help?"

"That really hurt."

"I'm here for you."

We *don't* need someone whose voice says things like this:

"If you had just listened to me, you wouldn't be in this jam."

"You know, life isn't fair. You need to grow up."

"Yeah, well, let me tell you how I was treated."

"Oh, come on. It wasn't that bad."

"You're too sensitive."

"I've got the solution for you."

"Hey, she was just having a bad day. Give her a break."

If you want to feel understood and validated, listen to the voices in the Psalms. Theologian Martin Marty observed that more than half of the psalms are "wintry," that is, they communicate the writer's heartache, despair, fear, hurt, and anger.[16] For instance, in Psalm 13, David wonders if God will ever come through for him again. Four times in two verses, he asks God, "How long?"

How long, LORD? Will you forget me forever?
How long will you hide your face from me?
How long must I wrestle with my thoughts and
day after day have sorrow in my heart?
How long will my enemy triumph
over me? —Psalm 13:1-2

> **Have you ever been that hurt, that angry? I have. We all have.**

And as an expression of raw anger, you can't find anything more validating than Psalm 109, which reads in part:

Appoint someone evil to oppose my enemy;
let an accuser stand at his right hand.
When he is tried, let him be found guilty,
and may his prayers condemn him.
May his days be few;
may another take his place of leadership....
But you, Sovereign LORD,
help me for your name's sake;

VOICES: The Power, Pain, & Purpose of Voices

out of the goodness of your love, deliver me.
For I am poor and needy,
and my heart is wounded within me.
—Psalm 109:6-8, 21-22

Have you ever been that hurt, that angry? I have. We all have. It doesn't do any good to insist that we're never hurt, afraid, or angry, or minimize the pain as "no big deal." We need to hear a voice that understands, empathizes, and sits with us while we process it all.

> We can be confused over any number of issues, relatively minor and very consequential.

WHEN WE'RE CONFUSED

As leaders, this is a place we avoid like the plague! We want to lead with clarity and boldness, cast a vision of a better future, and marshal all the people and resources to achieve it. But sometimes, we feel stuck. We don't know which way to turn, and we don't like feeling this way at all! In my work consulting with pastors and other leaders around the world, this is the place and the time when they ask me to come see them. They're not sure how to handle a difficult situation or, more likely, a difficult person. My first task is to understand, and if appropriate, validate their perceptions and feelings: "Yes, this is a sticky one. I can see why it's hard to decide which course to take."

When we're confused and we share our frustration with the wrong person, we may get a flood of advice: "You just need to do this or that," as if we hadn't thought of this or that dozens of times! Instead, we need someone to step into the quagmire with us, feel what we feel, and actively listen as we process the problem and the options in front of us. Let me share some scenarios:

» As senior leaders get older and "more seasoned," the voices in their heads about their end dates grow louder: "How long can I be effective in this role? What does succession look like? Who needs to be part of the process?" And a thousand other crucial questions. They want to be sure they leave a legacy of continued impact, but they inevitably need help clarifying the choices and finding the right path forward.

» All of us have had the misfortune of observing friends who are "going off the rails" in one way

VOICES: The Power, Pain, & Purpose of Voices

or another—strained and broken relationships, poor leadership decisions, unwillingness to take advice, and plenty of other possible problems. As we anticipate an honest conversation, competing voices ricochet in our minds: "If I say this, he'll say that. If I don't say anything, maybe he'll get over it on his own. If I wade in, I might make things worse."

» One of the most difficult challenges for many senior leaders is letting a staff member go. For months (and maybe years), we've tried to convince ourselves the problem isn't really that bad, and the flashes of competence will surely become normal. But the problem persists, and competence (or a better attitude) hasn't shown signs of progress. We want to give that person the benefit of the doubt, and we want to believe the best, but either poor performance or a poor attitude is dragging the team down. We can spend much of our time trying to sort out the right path to address personnel issues and time we need to invest in more productive ways. (For most readers, faces are appearing in your mind right now!)

» Sooner or later, every senior leader has to raise a considerable amount of money to propel the vision forward . . . or replace the roof and the

HVAC equipment. A flurry of questions fill our minds: "Do we really need it? How much will it cost? Can it be done less expensively? Where will we get the money? How can we raise it so it inspires people? How does this fit, or not fit, with our other capital campaigns?"

We can be confused over any number of issues, personal and professional, short-term and long-term, relatively minor and very consequential. When someone comes alongside to walk with us through the mud, we've found a true friend.

WHEN WE'RE INSPIRED

Ahhh, this is where we want to live . . . and stay. We have bursts of insight about situations that have been stuck for a long time, and we can't wait to move things forward. God gives us clear direction about a problem, and we're confident we now know what to do. We've worked hard on a project over a long period of time, and we see it bear fruit. When we see broken relationships mended and lost people found, tears come to our eyes. In these and countless other leadership moments, we're truly inspired. At these treasured times, what are the voices we need to hear?

VOICES: The Power, Pain, & Purpose of Voices

First, let me identify and illustrate the voices we *don't* need to hear:

» "That's great...I guess."

Other leaders may see us as competition, and they believe it's a zero-sum game: when we win, they lose. They see our success as a threat to their reputations. They don't come out and say it (and they may not be self-aware enough to recognize it), but they aren't that thrilled that we've achieved something significant. Their mouths speak praise, but their nonverbals say something else.

» "Wow, you're terrific!"

Sounds good, doesn't it? Broad, sweeping encouragement may be nice, but it doesn't touch the heart.

» "Good, but you could have done better."

As the saying goes, "Some people can find something wrong with a bowl of ice cream." They delight in picking things apart until they find something to criticize. Maybe they think it makes them look smart, or maybe it's a way to dominate or intimidate. Whatever the reason, it's not that helpful. Of course, honest feedback is essential, but those who want the best for us find ways to give feedback in ways that build us up instead of tearing us down.

So, what are the messages we need to hear when things are going well? We need others to:

» Be genuine.

Can you tell if someone's affirmation is heartfelt? Usually, but not always. I appreciate it when the person "leans in" to be sure to find the right words to fit me and the circumstances. It's not a flippant remark. In many cases, it's obvious they've thought and planned (at least for a minute or two) about how to say it.

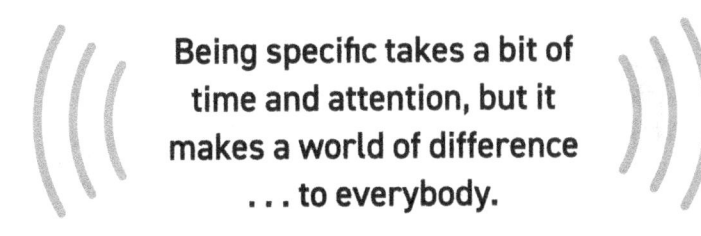

> **Being specific takes a bit of time and attention, but it makes a world of difference ... to everybody.**

» Be specific.

Instead of saying, "You're great!" it's far more powerful to identify the details of what we did well—the way we communicated with a particular person, the way we framed the need and the way we created an atmosphere that brought out the best in others.

Being specific takes a bit of time and attention, but it makes a world of difference ... to everybody. In an

VOICES: The Power, Pain, & Purpose of Voices

article in *Forbes* about helping others succeed, Amy Rees Anderson says that focusing on details is essential:

It lets them know that you truly care about their life. The more a person knows that you genuinely care about them, the more they will in turn move heaven and earth to help you with the things you want. And with the contact tracking tools available on our electronic devices today, it is incredibly simple to make quick notes about people so your memory can always be fresh."[17]

» Be forward-facing.

Affirmation of past accomplishments and impact easily leads to encouragement about the future. Again, this takes some thought to connect the dots to what might come next. Someone might say, "You did so well when you did this and that and this and that, and I can see you gaining confidence in using your God-given talents. I don't know what's over the next hill for you, but you're becoming a terrific leader, and the Lord may open doors for you to take on even more responsibility. You can do it. I've been watching, and I know it's true."

You and I are no different than all the people, famous and infamous, Oprah interviewed over the years. All of us wonder if we matter, and even more, if anyone else believes we matter. Thankfully, we can return again and

Voices We Long to Hear

again to the voice of God, who understands us to the core of our being and adores us. We hear Him say, "You are my beloved child. I delight in you. Others may forget you or take you for granted, but I never will. I have your name inscribed on my hand." Do you think that's going overboard? Look at what God said through Isaiah: "Can a mother forget the baby at her breast and have no compassion on the child she has borne? Though she may forget, I will not forget you! See, I have engraved you on the palms of my hands" (Isaiah 49:15-16).

Believe it. Soak in it. Let this voice melt you and mold you.

THINK ABOUT IT:

1) Does it amaze you that every person Oprah has interviewed asked if they did okay? Why?

2) What voice do you need to hear—and not need to hear—when you're angry?

3) What voice do you need to hear—and not need to hear—when you're hurt and afraid?

4) What voice do you need to hear—and not need to hear—when you're confused?

VOICES: The Power, Pain, & Purpose of Voices

5) What voice do you need to hear—and not need to hear—when you're inspired?

6) Think about the people you care about. What do they need to hear from you?

THE VOICE IN YOUR HEAD BECOMES THE VOICE IN YOUR MOUTH. THE VOICE IN YOUR MOUTH BECOMES THE VOICE IN OTHERS' HEADS.

CHAPTER 5

Micro-Voices

IT WAS SUCH A SMALL THING: THE METAL FRACTURE was only a tenth of an inch deep, not even noticeable, but during rush hour on December 15, 1967, the Silver Bridge over the Ohio River between Point Pleasant, West Virginia, and Gallipolis, Ohio, collapsed. Forty-six people died, and two of them were never recovered from the swirling, frigid water. The tiny fracture was the result of a design flaw in the eyebar-chain construction. For almost forty years since the bridge was completed, no one imagined there was anything wrong. Water from rain and snow and salt from years of clearing ice seeped into the crack, weakening the spot and putting added stress on other parts of the bridge. Gradually, imperceptibly, the load became too much of a strain, and the bridge tumbled into the river. Inspectors took three years to determine the cause of the catastrophe. The tragedy led the government to conduct regular inspections of bridges. Only two other bridges used the eyebar-chain method: one in Brazil and the other just upstream from the Silver Bridge at St. Mary's, West Virginia, which was immediately closed and soon demolished and replaced.[18]

This isn't just a tragic story; it's an analogy of what can (and often does) happen to leaders, and by extension, anyone who isn't living a stress-free life. (I think that's inclusive enough!) We don't even notice micro-stresses—communicated by micro-voices—until the cumulative damage is evident ... and disastrous. Consultant Thom Ranier has identified nine that are inherent in the role of a pastor and other church leaders, and each one applies to leaders in all organizations.[19] Sometimes, these stress points are communicated in whispers, and sometimes with shouts, but we hear each one. They apply to business leaders as well as pastors (again, with my commentary).

Micro-Voices

1) Voices during decision overload

Senior leaders are called on to make countless decisions every week—in staff meetings, board meetings, phone calls to people in need, answering a myriad of questions, the flow and content of messages, relating to visitors, caring for people in the hospital, making budget allocations, relating to people who find fault with almost anything, and many, many others. When these leaders get home at the end of an exhausting day, they're spent, mentally exhausted. When the spouse or one of the children asks a question, they don't even want to respond. One pastor told me his greatest challenge is "decision fatigue." If senior leaders only needed to make decisions in half of these cases, they wouldn't be stressed, but people look to them to make all of them... and to make the right decision each time.

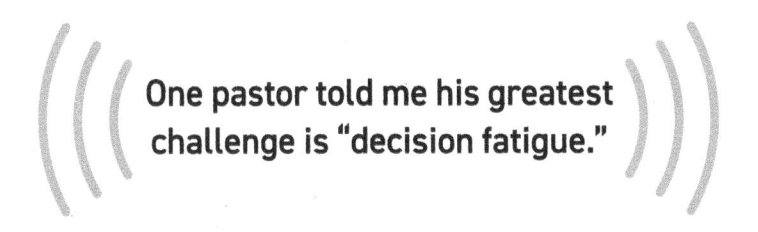

> **One pastor told me his greatest challenge is "decision fatigue."**

The voices, in our heads and in our ears, say, "You'd better not mess this one up!"

VOICES: The Power, Pain, & Purpose of Voices

2) Critical voices

We'd like to be immune to criticism, but we're not. We want to be seen as strong and confident, but some people know how to push our buttons. Sometimes, it's the unfairness of the comment that gets to us, but sometimes, it's the source. A few of us can listen, analyze the validity of the remarks, and learn from the interaction, but most of us take it too much to heart. We question our competence and our influence. Criticism is a little more salt and a little more water widening the crack and weakening our confidence structure.

The voices ask, "Who do you think you are?"

> **Criticism is a little more salt and a little more water widening the crack and weakening our confidence structure.**

3) Voices on an emotional rollercoaster

I'm well aware that business leaders face stresses that are just as severe as pastors do, but not in this area. Within the span of days, and maybe hours, we might celebrate with a couple over the birth of a child and then officiate at the funeral of a teenager who was killed in an accident. One pastor related that on a Tuesday he sat with a woman in shock after her husband committed suicide, on Wednesday he had to release an employee who had been on the team for twelve years, on Friday he had to call 911 because a man came to the church office with a gun, on Saturday he spoke at the funeral of a long-time friend, and on Sunday, he had to find the emotional strength to preach his heart out. Business executives can experience dramatic ups and downs—breaking sales records one day and losing a valued customer the next.

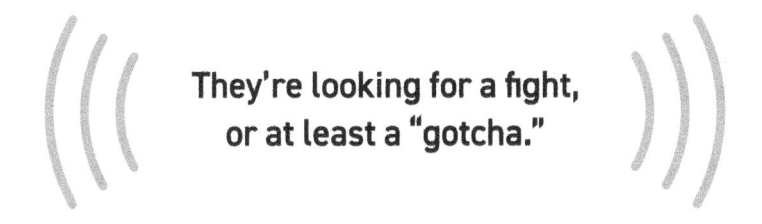

> **They're looking for a fight, or at least a "gotcha."**

The voices insist, "Come on. Just one more. If not you, who?"

VOICES: The Power, Pain, & Purpose of Voices

4) Voices demanding excellence ... all the time, in every way

Leading people—and for pastors, teaching God's truth—are the greatest pleasures of our role, and we eagerly welcome questions from people who are trying to grasp business principles or the meaning in passages of Scripture. But some people, it seems, aren't really looking for answers. They're looking for a fight, or at least a "gotcha." They've read this book or that article, listened to a podcast or had a conversation with a friend from a different part of God's family, and they're ready to challenge us ... and prove us wrong. It doesn't take many of these people to steal our joy and make us wonder if some of our teachings will come back to bite us.

The voices nag, "Have you studied enough? Really?"

5) Voices demanding us to be "always on"

This is different from the emotional extremes, though they overlap in many cases. No matter how much our churches have grown and no matter how many competent people are on our staff teams, all of us are still involved in pastoral care. We officiate at weddings and funerals, visit the sick, listen to the hurting, spend time making referrals to doctors and others who can help our people, and try to soothe the hurt feelings of those who are upset. The people around us experience all kinds of difficulties, and we're there to comfort and guide them through. This, of course, is on top of our other responsibilities to lead, administrate, plan, preach, and do all the other things on our lists. For business leaders, the list of demands may be different, but the list is there ... and the voices are just as demanding.

The voices wonder, "Where were you? Don't you care?"

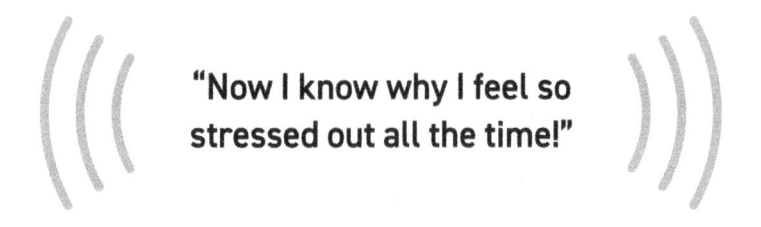

> "Now I know why I feel so stressed out all the time!"

6) Voices of deadlines

When we look at the schedule for a typical week, we see a host of deadlines. We have to prepare for this meeting and that one, show up on time for these people and those people, talk to team members about launching or shepherding programs assigned to them, and keep every project on track. And for pastors, the most conspicuous deadline is when we walk on stage

VOICES: The Power, Pain, & Purpose of Voices

to preach on Sunday morning. There's no hiding or delaying at that point!

The voices ask, "What have you forgotten?"

7) Voices of unrealistic expectations

At a retreat of about thirty senior leaders, the speaker asked, "What do people expect us to do well?" He asked someone to write the responses on a whiteboard. It didn't take long for the answers to pour out: finances, administration, leading the team, compassion, inspiring communication, and on and on. After the first few fairly global ones, they became more specific, such as, "My board expects me to be both a commanding, visionary, powerful leader and their best friend. I don't know how to be both at the same time." They kept throwing out answers until the whiteboard was completely full, with the last few written sideways in the little room that was left. Then, silence... except for the soft crying of a few people. The leader asked, "What's going on? What has touched you so much?" One person said, "Now I know why I feel so stressed out all the time!" Lots of heads nodded.

Our people expect us to be experts in everything. We're not. They look to us to solve every problem. We can't. They want us to meet every need. That's not possible. But their expectations are both a blessing and a curse. They're a blessing because they respect us and look to us for leadership, but they're a curse because we can only meet their expectations in a few areas of our best talents. A Florida pastor was asked to make it snow on Christmas Day. Honestly.

> **Our people expect us to be experts in everything. We're not.**

This is in addition to our own voice, which often insists on higher expectations of ourselves than anyone else.

The voices want to know, "Don't you have superpowers?"

8) Family voices

We know our priority list is God, family, and ministry, but God is invisible, and the ministry is always screaming for our attention, so our families often feel left out and ignored. One pastor remembered, "It's been over three decades, but I'm still haunted by the look on my little boy's face when I had to back out of

VOICES: The Power, Pain, & Purpose of Voices

our weekly lunch at McDonald's. A church member called to tell me that he and his wife were about to split up, and I needed to come because it was an emergency. I let my son down, and the guy's marriage failed. I wish I could say that was the only time I put ministry before my family. It's not."

The voices sneer, "How can you be so calloused?"

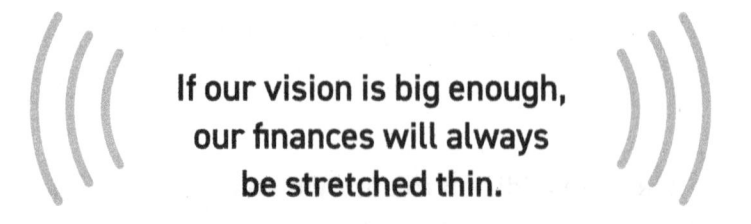

> **If our vision is big enough, our finances will always be stretched thin.**

9) Voices of financial strains

If our vision is big enough, our finances will always be stretched thin. That's part of the deal for leaders, and we can't wish it away. It's wise to put enough money into a contingency fund, but that's not a guarantee we won't worry about paying the bills. And of course, it's not only the church finances that stress us; we can have that pit in our stomachs when our own bank account hits zero before the month runs out of days. How are we going to pay for our kid's braces? And all the fees for playing on sports teams? And another car when they're old enough? And college tuition, housing, and books? A friend of mine was worried about how he could pay for college for his two children. One night he suddenly sat up in bed in a cold sweat. He told his startled wife, "What are we gonna do? I have no idea how we'll make this work."

The voices ask, "Did you get into the right line of work?"

We've looked at the statistics of more than five out of ten senior church leaders contemplating leaving the ministry because they're burned out and the stress is too much for them. How did they get to this point? They listened to whispers and shouts that eroded their confidence. These voices produced tiny cracks that gradually weakened their strength and resolve. Burnout doesn't happen all at once. Ernest Hemingway wrote the popular novel *The Sun Also Rises*, which follows the turbulent events in Spain after World War I. The book asks readers to peer into the lives of ex-pats who travel to Pamplona in Northern Spain for the festival of San Fermin and "the running of the bulls." The book is witty and unexpectedly layered, which I didn't fully appreciate when I first read it in high school. Hemingway's story brought the festival (and the bulls) to the attention of the English-speaking world. It has

VOICES: The Power, Pain, & Purpose of Voices

become the most popular internationally renowned celebration in Spain, with over a million people participating each year. Some mistakenly attribute one of the most famous quotes in the book to Mark Twain, but it's Hemingway's dialogue between two characters in his story:

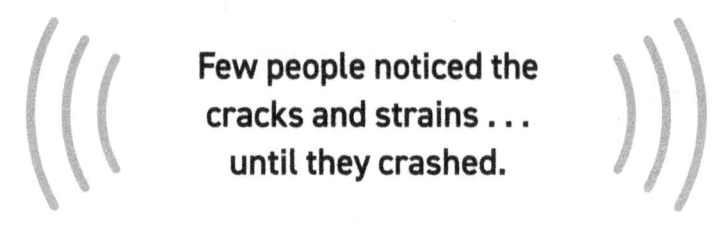

> **Few people noticed the cracks and strains . . . until they crashed.**

"How did you go bankrupt?" Bill asked.

"Two ways," Mike said. "Gradually and then suddenly."[20]

I've watched as leaders have tried to shoulder enormous stress for years. Few people noticed the cracks and strains . . . until they crashed. Who is watching what's gradually happening to you?

Like the government after the Silver Bridge collapse, we need to conduct regular and thorough inspections to observe any recent cracks in our steel construction. Hear the voices. Pay attention to them. They might lead you to one of the cracks so you can address the problem before it becomes a disaster.

Micro-Voices

What does an inspection look like for a leader? It probably includes regular physical checkups, consistent (at least quarterly) meetings with a consultant or a trusted peer who asks hard questions and doesn't let you off with simple answers, better delegation of responsibilities and follow-up, protected time with your spouse and children, and investing in a hobby or sport that relaxes you and gives you pleasure.

These stresses usually don't just go away, but they don't have to result in a disaster.

THINK ABOUT IT:

1) Which two or three of the powerful voices do you hear most often or most acutely?

2) Where are the voices coming from? How do they affect you?

3) How have you tried to manage them?

4) Write an inspection plan. Who will you choose as the chief inspector? How will implementing the plan affect your well-being, your most important relationships, and your leadership?

VOICES: The Power, Pain, & Purpose of Voices

THE VOICE IN YOUR HEAD BECOMES THE VOICE IN YOUR MOUTH. THE VOICE IN YOUR MOUTH BECOMES THE VOICE IN OTHERS' HEADS.

CHAPTER 6

Competing Voices

THE GREEK PHILOSOPHER AESOP USED A STORY TO warn us about competing voices:

A man and his son were once going with their donkey to market. As they were walking along by its side a countryman passed them and said: "You fools, what is a donkey for but to ride upon?"

So the man put the boy on the donkey and they went on their way. But soon they passed a group of men, one of whom said: "See that lazy youngster, he lets his father walk while he rides."

So the man ordered his boy to get off and got on himself. But they hadn't gone far when they passed two

VOICES: The Power, Pain, & Purpose of Voices

women, one of whom said to the other: "Shame on that lazy lout to let his poor little son trudge along."

Well, the man didn't know what to do, but at last, he took his boy up before him on the donkey. By this time they had come to the town, and the passers-by began to jeer and point at them. The man stopped and asked what they were scoffing at. The men said: "Aren't you ashamed of yourself for overloading that poor donkey of yours and your hulking son?"

The man and boy got off and tried to think what to do. They thought and they thought, till at last they cut down a pole, tied the donkey's feet to it, and raised the pole and the donkey to their shoulders. They went along amid the laughter of all who met them till they came to Market Bridge, when the donkey, getting one of his feet loose, kicked out and caused the boy to drop his end of the pole. In the struggle, the donkey fell over the bridge, and with his forefeet being tied together, he was drowned.

"That will teach you," said an old man who had followed them: Please all, and you will please none."[21]

Can you relate to the man in the story? I sure can. In almost every decision, I can identify several options . . . and often people I trust give me very different advice. If I'm not careful, I'll get stuck wondering what to do, and maybe do nothing . . . or try to do everything.

We're not alone. When we read the accounts of people in the Scriptures, we realize they heard competing voices too—often loud ones, sometimes whispered ones. It's instructive to recall what they faced.

> "You're a fool!" may have been the nicest comment they heard.

NOAH

God had had it. He had created the world and put mankind in it to represent him and flourish, but sin had polluted and ruined his plans . . . or so it seemed. God told Noah,

I am going to put an end to all people, for the earth is filled with violence because of them. I am surely going to destroy both them and the earth. So make yourself an ark of cypress wood; make rooms in it and coat it with pitch inside and out.
—*Genesis 6:13-14*

VOICES: The Power, Pain, & Purpose of Voices

God gave him detailed instructions, including the news that it wasn't just for Noah and his family—he was building a floating zoo!

Can you imagine the comments of his neighbors? (We already know they weren't the kind of people we'd like to live next door!) Throughout the 120 years of construction, they undoubtedly made fun of him and his sons as they built this monstrous boat ... on dry land. "You're a fool!" may have been the nicest comment they heard. Did Noah ever waver? The writer doesn't tell us that Noah doubted. It only says, "Noah did everything just as God commanded him" (Genesis 6:22). Noah resisted the mocking voices and followed through with the strange directions God had given him.

ABRAHAM

When he was seventy-five years old, God spoke to Abraham (Abram at the time) and told him to leave his homeland with his wife and nephew Lot. I would have asked, "Well, okay, this is a surprise. Where do you want us to go?" No reply from God to this reasonable question. Instead, God announced one of the most momentous promises in the Bible:

> *I will make you into a great nation, and I will bless you; I will make your name great, and you will be a blessing. I will bless those who bless you, and*

whoever curses you I will curse; and all peoples on earth will be blessed through you. —Genesis 12:2-3

The little group hiked all the way from Ur to Syria, then to Egypt, and finally to Canaan—over 2,000 miles—and God again appeared to Abraham: "To your offspring, I will give this land" (Genesis 12:7). I can imagine asking God, "That's great. When?" No reply.

> **I can imagine the conversations in the tent between the two old travelers!**

Years went by, but Abraham and Sarah still didn't have a child. Eventually, Abraham gave up. He decided to give his inheritance (and the promise) to Eliezer of Damascus. It looked like Abraham had come to a dead end, but God said, "Not so fast!" (Or words to that effect.) "Look up at the sky and count the stars—if indeed you can count them ... So shall your offspring be" (Genesis 15:5).

VOICES: The Power, Pain, & Purpose of Voices

Abraham had been telling himself, "Look at my old, tired body... and Sarah!" But God said, "Look at the stars... and look to me! I'll fulfill my promise—not in the way or the timing you expect but in my way and my timing."

Soon after this dramatic moment when God confirmed His promise with a covenant, Sarah gave up. She decided the only way God could make it happen was through her maid, Hagar. I can imagine the conversations in the tent between the two old travelers! Abraham, sometimes not the bravest of men, gave in, and Hagar had a son, Ishmael.

Another dramatic voice came to Abraham later. Three men approached him. As they ate together, one of the visitors announced, "I will surely return to you about this time next year, and Sarah your wife will have a son." Sarah had been eavesdropping, and couldn't help but laugh. She told herself, "After I am worn out and my lord is old, will I now have this pleasure?" But God affirmed this updated and more specific version of the promise (Genesis 18:10, 12). And a year later, Isaac was born.

We'll look at one more set of competing voices for Abraham. When Isaac was twelve, God again spoke to the old father, and this time, it wasn't a promise, it was a test: "Take your son, your only son, whom you love—Isaac—and go to the region of Moriah. Sacrifice him there as a burnt offering on a mountain I will show you" (Genesis 22:2).

We don't get a glimpse of the awful struggle that must have gone through Abraham's mind and heart, but we can imagine him praying, "What? This can't be right! Kill him? Don't you remember all we went through to get here?"

But the very next morning, Abraham loaded a donkey with wood for a sacrifice and set off with his son and two servants. When they arrived on the third day (and every step must have been torture for the old man), Abraham told the men to stay behind while he took Isaac, the wood, a torch, and a knife up the mountain. Isaac asked, "The fire and wood are here ... but where is the lamb for the burnt offering?"

Abraham's heart must have been torn to pieces at that moment, but he responded, "God himself will provide the lamb for the burnt offering, my son" (Genesis 22:7-8).

In one of the most gut-wrenching scenes in the Bible, Abraham built an altar, tied up Isaac, and put him on the wood. He picked up his knife to complete the mission God had given him. In the movie *The Bible*, George C. Scott plays Abraham. The screenwriter has Isaac look up at his father at this moment and ask,

VOICES: The Power, Pain, & Purpose of Voices

"There is nothing that He may not ask of thee?" And Abraham says simply, "Nothing."[22] This dialogue isn't in Genesis, but it perfectly captures Abraham's intense inner conflict.

At that moment, Abraham heard the voice of the angel of the Lord who stopped the knife from doing its work. I'm not sure who was more relieved, the old man or his son. God provided a ram for the sacrifice that day, and the two walked back home.

> Abraham's life was full of competing and conflicting voices.

Abraham's life was full of competing and conflicting voices. Sometimes he listened to the wrong ones, but in the critical moments, he followed God's leading.

JOSEPH

Few people have suffered such lows or enjoyed such highs. When Joseph was a boy, he had two dreams that his brothers and even his parents would someday bow down to him. That's an incredible message for the eleventh son in a patriarchal culture that rewards the oldest son... but it might have been smart to keep the dreams to himself. When he told his family, his brothers were furious, and his father was incredulous. His brothers plotted to do away with their arrogant pest of a brother, so when he showed up miles from home to check up on them (Jacob must not have realized what was going on with his boys!), they threw him in a pit and sold him as a slave to a passing caravan headed to Egypt. The voice of his brothers said, "We're making sure you're never coming home!"

You know the rest of the story, but listen to the voices Joseph heard:

Potiphar said, "You're really good at managing things. I'm putting you in charge of everything!"

But his wife said, "You're really handsome. Come to bed with me!"

Joseph said, "Not gonna happen."

Potiphar said, "Well, you can't stay here. To prison with you."

The warden said, "Hey, where did you get your talents? I'm putting you in charge."

The cupbearer and baker said, "Can you interpret our dreams?"

Pharoah said, "How about mine?"

VOICES: The Power, Pain, & Purpose of Voices

The brothers showed up and said, "Can we have something to eat?"

Joseph said, "Hey guys, it's me!"

His dad said, "Is it really you?"

Joseph told his brothers, "I forgive you. God sent me here for your sake."

The voices he heard ranged from high praise to fierce hatred, but the voices he spoke were confident in God's sovereign plan, no matter how things looked at any moment.

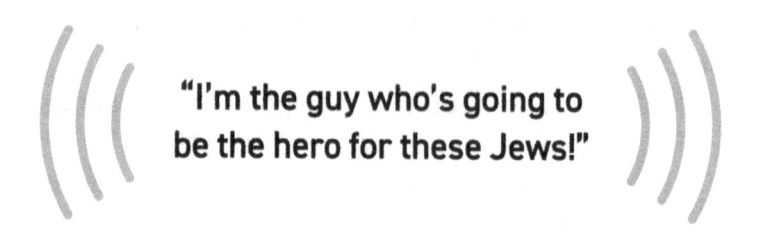

> "I'm the guy who's going to be the hero for these Jews!"

MOSES

When he lived in Pharaoh's court, Moses' inner voices must have told him, "I'm the guy who's going to be the hero for these Jews!" But after he murdered an Egyptian, his self-talk changed. He became a wandering outcast, not the leader of a great movement... not for forty years, anyway. At the burning bush, he heard

God's voice. Instead of being cocky, he needed God's prodding to do what he commanded.

Moses spoke boldly to Pharoah, watched as plagues devastated the land, and led the exodus toward the Promised Land. On the way, he heard voices of criticism and doubt—and the sounds of the party with the golden calf! The burden of leading these people felt overwhelming, but he kept plodding forward. In the end, he didn't make it into the land of promise because he didn't obey God's voice—he struck the rock in anger. God provided water for the people, but Moses wasn't allowed to enter the land.

Moses was a man of competing voices, his own and the people he led.

JOSHUA AND CALEB

When God chose Joshua to lead the people from the wilderness into Canaan, he spoke words of confidence and challenge:

Be strong and very courageous. Be careful to obey all the law my servant Moses gave you; do not turn from it to the right or to the left, that you may be successful wherever you go. Keep this Book of the Law always on your lips; meditate on it day and night, so that you may be careful to do everything written in it. Then you will be prosperous

VOICES: The Power, Pain, & Purpose of Voices

and successful. Have I not commanded you? Be strong and courageous. Do not be afraid; do not be discouraged, for the LORD your God will be with you wherever you go. —Joshua 1:7-9

During the conquest, he led the people into the miracle at Jericho and the debacle at Ai. There were dramatic moments, like crossing the Jordan on the dry riverbed, and months and years of grinding warfare. Through it all, Joshua led with integrity.

"Give me that hill country!"

Joshua and Caleb were the two spies who gave a good report forty years before finally entering the land. By this time, both were old men, but Caleb wasn't ready to sit on his porch in a rocking chair. His courage was as strong as ever. Some of God's people took the plains and valleys where crops would grow easily, but Caleb asked for land that was fiercely defended but not very good for farming. He remembered that Moses had told him, "The land on which your feet have walked will be your inheritance and that of your children forever, because you have followed the LORD my God wholeheartedly" (Joshua 14:9). And now, he claimed that land as his own:

> Now then, just as the LORD promised, he has kept me alive for forty-five years since the time he said this to Moses, while Israel moved about in the wilderness. So here I am today, eighty-five years old! I am still as strong today as the day Moses sent me out; I'm just as vigorous to go out to battle now as I was then. Now give me this hill country that the LORD promised me that day. You yourself heard then that the Anakites were there and their cities were large and fortified, but, the LORD helping me, I will drive them out just as he said.
> —Joshua 14:10-12

His eighty-five-year-old body may have shouted, "Take it easy!" But Caleb responded, "Give me that hill country!"

DAVID

Ignored by his parents, despised by his brothers... David didn't hear many positive voices when he was growing up. He became, at best, an errand boy to take supplies from his dad to his brothers, but when he

VOICES: The Power, Pain, & Purpose of Voices

showed up, he heard very loud and conflicting voices. Goliath yelled insults against God and God's army, but when David expressed outrage, his brothers made fun of him. King Saul didn't have much confidence in the boy to defeat the giant, but since no one else would fight him, he let David have a shot.

After the colossal victory over Goliath and the enemy, David heard people praise him... at Saul's expense. Suddenly the praises were coupled with an attempt by the king to nail David to the wall with a spear!

For the rest of his life, David heard haunting voices of opposition, especially from his son Absalom and other rebels, but he also spoke beautiful songs of love, hope, and faith in the Psalms.

ELIJAH

Oh man, what was going on in this guy's mind? Elijah had played the starring role in one of the most dramatic events in the Bible: the contest between God and the prophets of Baal on Mt. Carmel. The people who watched fire fall from heaven when the prophet prayed were stunned. If you've ever had a successful event (and you've had many, I'm sure), you have at least a taste of the euphoria of seeing God do something magnificent. His faith must have been rock solid and sky-high!

Competing Voices

But in a flash, everything changed for him:
Now Ahab told Jezebel everything Elijah had done and how he had killed all the prophets with the sword. So Jezebel sent a messenger to Elijah to say, "May the gods deal with me, be it ever so severely, if by this time tomorrow I do not make your life like that of one of them."

How did the faith-filled prophet respond to this threatening voice? "Elijah was afraid and ran for his life." He ran into the wilderness, sat down under a tree, and prayed, "I have had enough, LORD. Take my life" (1 Kings 19:1-4).

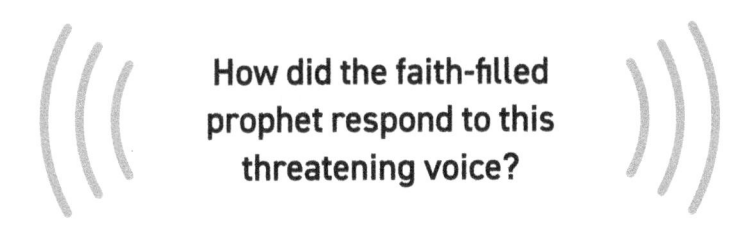

> **How did the faith-filled prophet respond to this threatening voice?**

Psychologists tell us that we're often vulnerable to self-doubt after a major success. That's what we see here. Elijah's inner critic must have been running in high gear!

VOICES: The Power, Pain, & Purpose of Voices

But another voice came to the depressed, isolated prophet: The angel of the Lord spoke to him two times and provided food, water, and rest. The third time, God entered into dialogue with Elijah. God told him to stand on the mountain in his presence, and then... A great wind "tore the mountains apart and shattered the rocks before the LORD."—that's some wind! But God wasn't in the wind. Then an earthquake shook the land under Elijah's feet, but God wasn't in the dramatic shaking. Then a fire consumed the area, but God wasn't in the fire (1 Kings 19:11, author paraphrase).

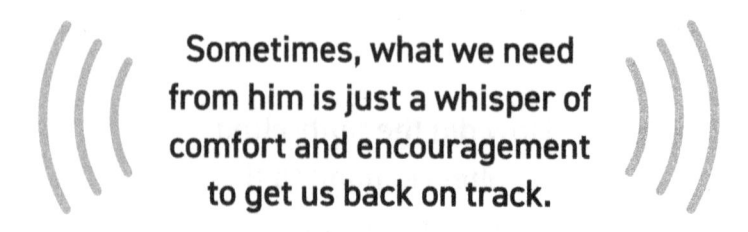

> Sometimes, what we need from him is just a whisper of comfort and encouragement to get us back on track.

I can imagine that Elijah had a flashback to the moment on Mt. Carmel when God showed up in shattering rocks and blazing fire, but this was different. God's voice came to the distraught and confused prophet in a gentle whisper, reinforcing his calling and giving him directions for continued ministry.

As leaders, we want to see God do dramatic, wonderful things to help us lead with courage and kindness, reveal his love and power, and change lives, but sometimes, what we need from Him is just a whisper of comfort and encouragement to get us back on track.

PAUL

If there has ever been a "come to Jesus moment" in anyone's life, it was Paul's. Actually, it was just the opposite: Jesus came to him! Before that pivotal moment when he heard Jesus' voice and saw a vision of the risen Christ, Paul had been a terror to Christians. In one of Luke's accounts of Paul's testimony, he tells King Agrippa:

I too was convinced that I ought to do all that was possible to oppose the name of Jesus of Nazareth. And that is just what I did in Jerusalem. On the authority of the chief priests I put many of the Lord's people in prison, and when they were put to death, I cast my vote against them. Many a time I went from one synagogue to another to have them punished, and I tried to force them to blaspheme. I was so obsessed with persecuting them that I even hunted them down in foreign cities. —Acts 26:9-11

VOICES: The Power, Pain, & Purpose of Voices

But on the road to Damascus, everything changed for Paul. His life became a catalog of miracles and suffering. The Spirit led him on his journeys to tell people the Good News, and when he was being taken to Rome as a prisoner because he had appealed to Caesar to hear his case, an angel spoke to him to assure him the people on the ship would be saved from the storm. Paul's voice was heard in the major cities of the Empire, and the church was established throughout the Roman world. His voice, through his letters, enables him to speak to us today, to inspire faith, to encourage repentance, and to call us to follow the Savior he followed.

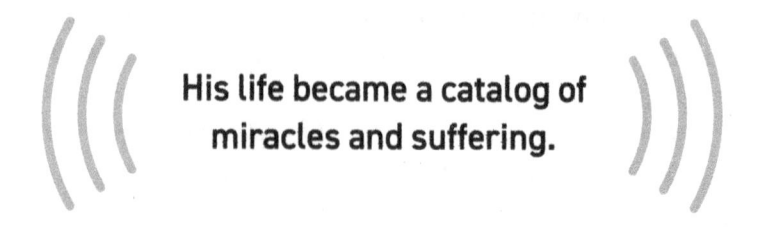

> His life became a catalog of miracles and suffering.

JESUS

At His baptism, Jesus heard the Father speak with a voice of supreme affirmation, "At that moment heaven was opened, and he saw the Spirit of God descending like a dove and alighting on him. And a voice from heaven said, 'This is my Son, whom I love; with him I am well pleased'" (Matthew 3:16-17). But soon, Jesus heard the voice of the deceiver. In the wilderness, Satan and Jesus battled over power and truth. In three temptations, Jesus quoted the Scriptures to refute the lies, ending with, "Away from me, Satan! For it is written: 'Worship the Lord your God, and serve him only'" (Matthew 4:10).

Throughout his ministry, the voice of the self-righteous, condemning religious leaders competed with Jesus' teaching of truth, faith, love, and obedience. In John's Gospel, we see them fiercely debate, with Jesus responding to their accusations with truth.

On Palm Sunday, the King of kings rode into Jerusalem on a donkey's colt, and the people shouted, "Hosanna! Blessed is he who comes in the name of the Lord! Blessed is the king of Israel!" (John 12:13) It was, in some ways, the pinnacle of His life and ministry—He was finally being recognized as the Messiah. But that day, He heard competing voices again. John tells us,

Now the crowd that was with him when he called Lazarus from the tomb and raised him from the dead continued to spread the word. Many people, because they had heard that he had performed this sign, went out to meet him. So the Pharisees said to one another, 'See, this is getting us

VOICES: The Power, Pain, & Purpose of Voices

nowhere. Look how the whole world has gone after him!'"—John 12:17-19

As a bookend of Jesus' ministry, just after the Triumphal Entry, some Greeks told Philip they wanted to meet Jesus. Jesus was troubled at the prospect of taking the sins of the world on Himself. He prayed, "Now my soul is troubled, and what shall I say? 'Father, save me from this hour'? No, it was for this very reason I came to this hour. Father, glorify your name!" (John 12:27-28)

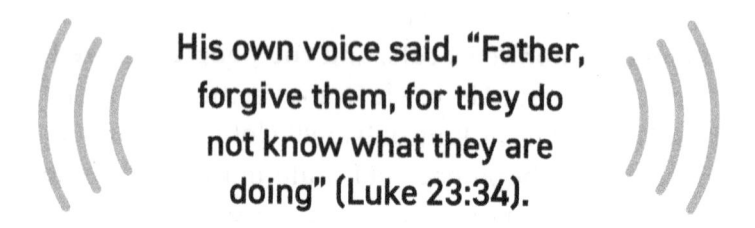

> His own voice said, "Father, forgive them, for they do not know what they are doing" (Luke 23:34).

At that moment, a voice from heaven assured him, "I have glorified it, and will glorify it again" (John 12:28).

On the cross, Jesus saw the grief and heard the sobs of the women and John who stood near Him, but He also heard the voices of those who jeered Him and mocked him... even as He died in their place, to bear the burden of their sins. His own voice said, "Father, forgive them, for they do not know what they are doing" (Luke 23:34).

We could have looked in detail at many others who heard conflicting voices, for instance:

» Hanun listened to advice from people in his palace, misunderstood David's intentions, and started a war (see 2 Samuel 10).

» Rehoboam ignored the wise voices of the elders, listened to the wrong people, and raised taxes, leading to the split between Israel and Judah (see 1 Kings 12).

» Job's wife and his "friends" blamed him for his troubles.

» Ahasuerus, emperor of Persia and Media, listened to everyone who entered his throne room, including his princes, Haman, Esther, and Mordecai.

» Nehemiah heard voices of opposition from his allies and his enemies.

» Peter had spoken too much and too soon before Jesus was arrested, and he denied even knowing Him when the chips were down. But Jesus wasn't finished with the fisherman. They met on the shore of the Sea of Galilee early one morning, and Jesus spoke words of truth, both to remind Peter

VOICES: The Power, Pain, & Purpose of Voices

of his biggest failure and restore him to participate in Jesus' mission. Jesus' voice that morning was the turning point in Peter's life.

As leaders, we hear conflicting voices. Some come from our best friends, others who love us, and from the Word itself, but others are spoken by those who mock and despise us or perhaps try to manipulate us with lies. We are in the world but not of the world—our job, every minute of every day, is to discern between the conflicting voices.

THINK ABOUT IT:

1) Which of these leaders do you identify with most closely? Why?

2) What were the conflicting voices the person you identified in Question 1 heard and said?

3) What are the ones you hear and say?

4) What are the conflicting voices on your team and in your church or organization today?

Competing Voices

THE VOICE IN YOUR HEAD BECOMES THE VOICE IN YOUR MOUTH. THE VOICE IN YOUR MOUTH BECOMES THE VOICE IN OTHERS' HEADS.

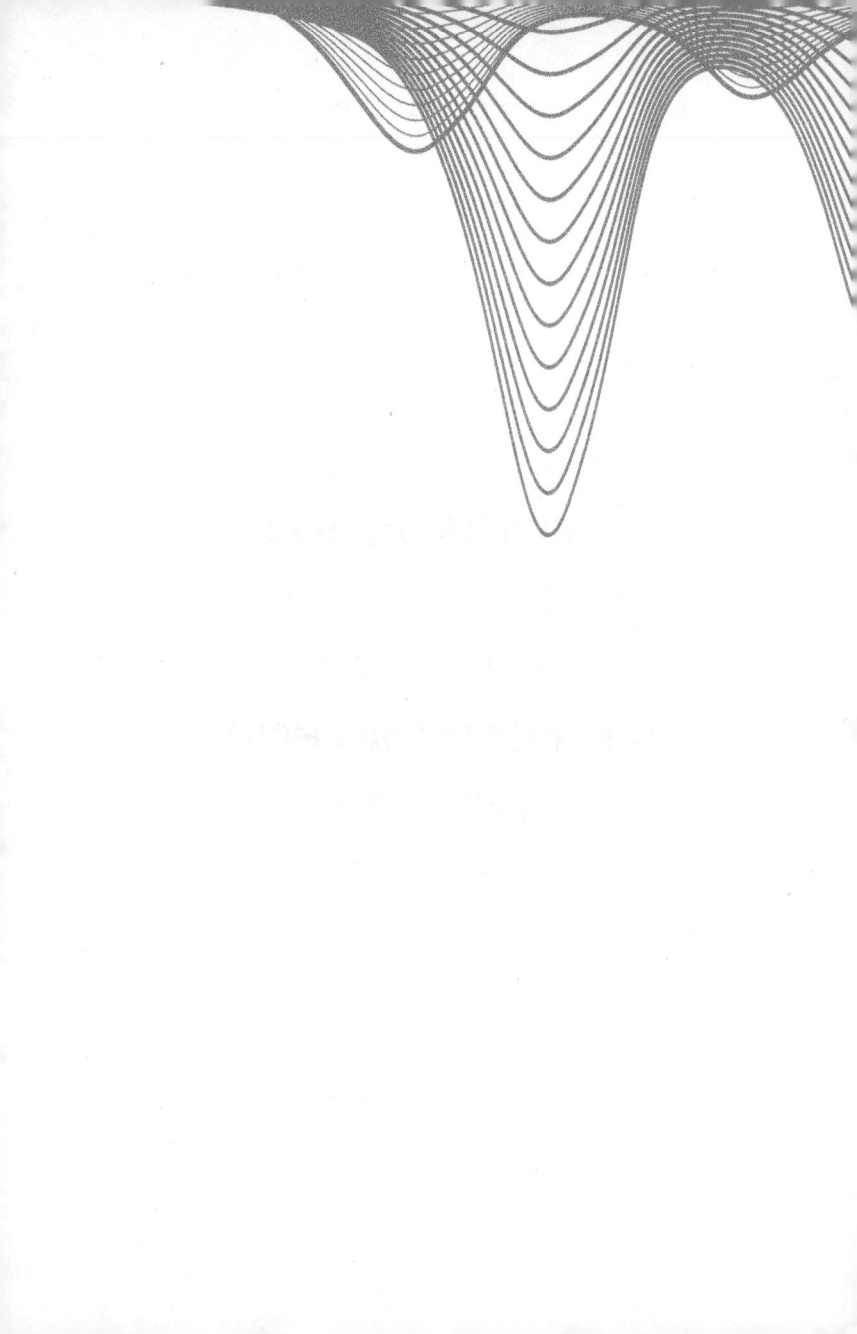

CHAPTER 7

Screening the Voices

A FEW YEARS AGO, WE EXITED "THE AGE OF TECH-nology" and entered "The Information Age." If that was true a decade or two ago, today we must be in "the hyper-information age." In 2007, the Yankelovich research firm surveyed more than 4,000 people about their online experiences, and they found that the average person was exposed to up to 5,000 ads every day. Today, the number has doubled to 10,000 ads per day, and that doesn't count the ones on television, radio, billboards, and other places where companies try to convince us to buy their products or use their

VOICES: The Power, Pain, & Purpose of Voices

services.[23] There are so many offers that we don't even notice the vast majority of them.

Ads have a surface promise and a deeper one. For instance, the surface promise of toothpaste is that it will clean your teeth, but that's not much of an attraction. The deeper promise is that the particular brand of toothpaste will make you more popular, you'll have more friends, and you'll find the love of your life. Now, that sizzles! Investment firm ads aren't just about managing retirement funds; they promise you'll be happy and healthy, and you'll travel the world. Ads for internet services don't just promise fast speeds and reliable connections; they'll give you more fulfillment than you ever dreamed possible! You get the idea. Next time you see an ad, ask yourself: *What's the surface promise, and what's the deeper one?* The enticing voices of these ads are more attractive than just the product or service.

The "voices" trying to get our attention aren't just ads. Adults under forty-five send and receive an average of more than eighty-five texts each day. Consumers of all ages send three messages per hour, a total of seventy-two each day.[24] (So if you think it's only "the young people" who are addicted to texting and social media, think again.)

Screening the Voices

Technology has radically changed the nature of communication. Texting has become the most popular way to connect, with about 30 percent of people willing to give up calling and use only texting to communicate.[25] Only a couple of generations ago, the number of communications people experienced was far less. They read the newspaper, listened to the radio, and talked to their family and friends. Today, corporations grab every chance to capture our attention, politicians try to convince us they're good, noble, and right and the other side is evil, bloggers explain everything under the sun, we have a vast array of news sources, online articles may or may not be tethered to any concept of truth, and churches try to compete with all this. We wonder why people are so distracted and have such short attention spans... and these are the ones God has commissioned to turn the world upside down!

> **One of the most important tasks is separating the noise from what's truly meaningful.**

VOICES: The Power, Pain, & Purpose of Voices

One of the most important tasks for each person today, and especially for leaders, is to learn how to screen the unimportant voices from the vital ones, separating the noise from what's truly meaningful. It's not easy, but it's necessary. Let me offer a few suggestions.

1) Learn to Listen

Solomon knew the value of listening. He wrote:

The way of fools seems right to them,
but the wise listen to advice.
—Proverbs 12:15

To answer before listening—that is folly and shame.
—Proverbs 18:13

Fools find no pleasure in understanding but
delight in airing their own opinions.
—Proverbs 18:2

We live in an instant society, and we expect everything to happen immediately (if not sooner!). If we jump to conclusions, we won't understand people, and our relationships will be transactional. That's fine in a drive-thru when we're picking up lunch, but not with people we love and lead.

Screening the Voices

When we slow down to listen, we ask second and third questions, inviting the person to explain more. The goal isn't just adding to our understanding of the person's concepts, though that's important; we also communicate that we value the person enough to engage at a deeper level.

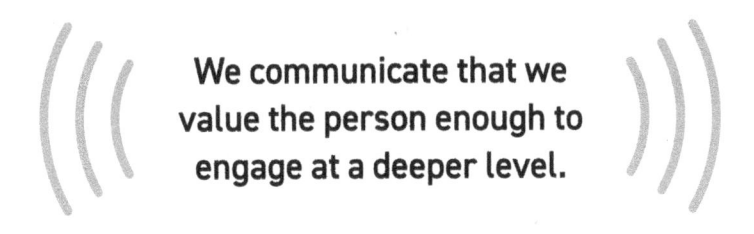

> **We communicate that we value the person enough to engage at a deeper level.**

Far too often, people spend too much time listening to unproductive voices, like endless YouTube videos about who-knows-what, and not enough time investing in face-to-face and heart-to-heart conversations.

What are some ways you can tell if your interactions are more transactional than relational?

2) Make Fewer Assumptions

In theology, politics, sports, and every other part of life that draws out the passions of people, we tend to listen to sources that already agree with us. We filter

VOICES: The Power, Pain, & Purpose of Voices

what we allow into our lives using "confirmation bias," and we're at least suspicious, if not downright hostile, to anyone who disagrees with us. This is not the way to become wise, it's not the way to build bridges, and it's not the way to get to know people.

> **Taking sides has always been part of the human condition, but today, we've elevated it to exclude and despise people God loves.**

It's human nature to want to belong, to have an identity as a member of a group we value. There's nothing wrong with being a Presbyterian or a Pentecostal, supporting one candidate or another, having differing views about economic policies, or rooting for our team, but when we can't hear opposing views without being defensive, angry, and condemning, we've crossed the line. We don't have to agree to be respectful; we can be respectful even if people cheer for our opponents.

Screening the Voices

Taking sides has always been part of the human condition, but today, we've elevated it to exclude and despise people God loves. No, I'm not going soft on biblical truth and values, but remember that Jesus went out of His way to connect with prostitutes and Pharisees. No one was off limits; no one was beyond the reach of His love. In the introduction to perhaps His most famous parable, The Prodigal Son, Luke takes us to the scene: "Now the tax collectors and sinners were all gathering around to hear Jesus. But the Pharisees and the teachers of the law muttered, 'This man welcomes sinners and eats with them'" (Luke 15:1-2). Imagine being there—Jesus, the perfect Son of God, was hanging out with the dregs of society when the arrogant religious leaders walked up and, in a stage whisper, condemned Jesus and His new friends. In that culture, eating with someone symbolized equality and acceptance. Jesus was doing what these leaders couldn't conceive of doing: treating outsiders with love and respect. They assumed the people sitting with Jesus weren't worthy of acceptance—or even tolerance, but Jesus assumed even the worst people were worthy of His love.

VOICES: The Power, Pain, & Purpose of Voices

3) Choose Sources Wisely

We're foolish to listen to the voices of people who don't have a track record of integrity. What is the person known for? What effect does he or she have on others? Does the person or organization traffic in extremes, or is there value for differences and nuances?

> **Their depth of experience, humility, and wisdom draw me to them. To me, their voices are treasures.**

Over the years, I've had the privilege to spend time with people I deeply respect. I go to them for advice because they've earned my trust. In many cases, they've been through the fires of difficulties, and they've learned lessons the hard way. Their depth of experience, humility, and wisdom draw me to them. To me, their voices are treasures.

4) Notice the Impact

Even if we don't know someone very well, we often can see their immediate impact on others. Some voices inspire, some comfort, and some give clear direction, but others cause confusion and division. I've met leaders at conferences and other events who I could tell had the love and respect of the people around them. They didn't lead with arrogance and demands; they led with genuine love and strength.

Good and godly voices inspire people to deeper faith and higher achievement. They draw out the best in others and see potential where others may not. But they don't insist on loyalty first to themselves; they consistently point people to the One who deserves their love and loyalty.

> **Inspiring voices help people identify and fine-tune their mission in life.**

VOICES: The Power, Pain, & Purpose of Voices

Inspiring voices help people identify and fine-tune their mission in life. They aren't just cogs in our success machine. They're people with God-given talents and dreams. Those who genuinely inspire take time to listen to those desires, affirm strengths, and celebrate growth and progress—even when that progress takes them to another organization.

"POSITIVE AFFECTIVE PRESENCE"

If we've learned to screen the voices we listen to, we'll be equipped to be the kind of voice that inspires others. In a *Harvard Business Review* article, Yale management professor Emma Seppälä and her collaborator Kim Cameron of the University of Michigan researched "the secret to successful leadership." They found that the single most significant predictor of success is not "charisma, influence, or power. It is not personality, attractiveness, or innovative genius. The one thing that supersedes all these factors is positive relational energy: the energy exchanged between people that helps uplift, enthuse, and renew them." They call this trait "positive affective presence": *positive*, because it's encouraging and hopeful; *affective*, because it has a powerful emotional component; and *presence*, because the trait's power is found in meaningful time spent with others. Beyond their academic research into this

Screening the Voices

topic, they recognize that all of us have felt the influence of people like this: "You've met people like this. They're like the sun. These people walk into a room and make it glow. Everyone becomes energized, enthused, inspired, and connected. These incandescent people are positive energizers."

Seppälä and Cameron divided people into "suns" and "energy sinks"—those whose presence brings light and warmth and those who "suck the air out of the room": some energize those near them and some "are just annoying."[26]

> **Screening some voices in and screening others out requires wisdom, diligence, and some good benchmarks to tell which ones are worth our attention.**

Energy without empathy doesn't have the same effect. The sun (to use their metaphor) doesn't just provide power, but it also gives needed warmth.

VOICES: The Power, Pain, & Purpose of Voices

It's certainly possible for leaders to exhibit warmth without energy, leaving the people they lead feeling cared for but not directed or motivated. And it's possible for leaders to have a lot of energy but lacking in kindness and compassion, perhaps impressing people with their drive but leaving a lot of people in their wake as they speed by. Inspiring voices do both—provide energy and empathy.

Screening some voices *in* and screening others *out* requires wisdom, diligence, and some good benchmarks to tell which ones are worth our attention. In one of Paul's letters to the Christians in Corinth (who famously had a lot of trouble figuring out who to listen to!), he provides a military metaphor to show the stakes involved in screening voices. He wrote,

For though we live in the world, we do not wage war as the world does. The weapons we fight with are not the weapons of the world. On the contrary, they have divine power to demolish strongholds. We demolish arguments and every pretension that sets itself up against the knowledge of God, and we take captive every thought to make it obedient to Christ.—2 Corinthians 10:3-5

What is Paul saying to us? We live in a messy, fallen world, so we can expect plenty of competing voices,

Screening the Voices

but God has given us weapons for the struggle. With His truth and grace, we can identify the strongholds of the inner critic, comparison, and condemnation, and "demolish" them. This means we don't dabble with them, and we don't give them space in our minds. We deal with them ruthlessly. We're exposed to "pretensions" all the time, voices that tell us God doesn't care, we're on our own, and nothing good can come of our circumstances. We need to pluck these voices of despair out of our thoughts and bring them into the light of Christ.

For us as leaders (and their followers), screening the voices we hear isn't optional. We need to acquire the skills and the experience to screen them well.

THINK ABOUT IT:

1) What are some of the most common ads you see? What's their surface message? What is their real promise?

2) Why is confirmation bias so attractive? What damage does it do?

VOICES: The Power, Pain, & Purpose of Voices

3) What are the most important and effective ways you screen the voices that come into your life?

4) How would you describe "positive affective presence"? Who has that role in your life? How well are you being that kind of leader?

5) Paul encourages us to be observant, objective, and even a bit obsessive about screening the messages that come to us. How can you apply the principles he shares?

THE VOICE IN YOUR HEAD BECOMES THE VOICE IN YOUR MOUTH. THE VOICE IN YOUR MOUTH BECOMES THE VOICE IN OTHERS' HEADS.

CHAPTER 8

Questioning Voices

GREAT LEADERS ASK GREAT QUESTIONS; POOR LEADERS assume they already know the answers. Leadership expert Peter Drucker observed, "The most serious mistakes are not being made as a result of wrong answers. The true dangerous thing is asking the wrong question." Mathematics and engineering professor Charles Steinmetz quipped, "There are no foolish questions, and no man [or woman] becomes a fool until he has stopped asking questions."[27]

One of the biggest compliments anyone has given me is, "Sam, you ask really good questions. They make me think more deeply than before." We live in

VOICES: The Power, Pain, & Purpose of Voices

a culture of instant information. We barely have time to type a question before Google gives us millions of answers! But reflection is vital for leaders to develop real wisdom. Let's look at questions we need to ask about ourselves, our leaders, and our organizations.

QUESTIONS FOR YOU

At least once a month, ask yourself these questions:

"What voice have I given too much space in my head?"

We all have at least one or two voices that beat us down, create self-doubt, and make us wonder if we have what it takes. The problem is that this voice sounds so familiar, so convincing, that we don't realize the damage it's doing.

"What voices speak life into me?"

Hopefully, we have several of these. It may be a spouse, a trusted friend, or a mentor who knows what makes you tick, sees your warts, and still believes in you. You may find an author or two whose message resonates in your soul, or you may find a powerful blend of comfort and passion by listening to a particular speaker or pastor. Are you giving time to these voices, or are they being squeezed out of your busy schedule?

Questioning Voices

> **Are you giving time to these voices, or are they being squeezed out of your busy schedule?**

"What voices create self-doubt?"

Some people assume self-doubt and humility are the same thing, or at least, very similar. In fact, they're poles apart. All of us have nagging voices that remind us of failures, rejection, times we've let others down, and times they've let us down. We can't do anything about these voices until we realize their destructive power, reject them, and replace them with positive affirmations about the unconditional love, forgiveness, and acceptance of God. Humble people still have those negative voices, but they're winning the battle. Instead of thinking about themselves and being involved in image management all the time, they can rest in their secure, loving relationship with God ... and keep fighting the battle in their minds and hearts.

VOICES: The Power, Pain, & Purpose of Voices

> Some people assume self-doubt and humility are the same thing, or at least, very similar. In fact, they're poles apart.

"What am I doing to move our team and our organization forward?"

Think of your past week. What meetings, decisions, and plans were productive and inspired the people around you? It's easy to take all your time with scheduled meetings and cover the same things over and over. Identify the few times, places, and people whose impact really made a difference and give your all to them.

"What is accelerating my growth as a leader?"

If you want your organization to grow and your team to develop, you need to be in the process, too. What are you doing to affirm your rock-solid identity in Christ? How are you setting and managing your priorities? How do you define success? What skills do you need to sharpen? What concepts need to be studied? What resources can help you be more effective? Invest in these.

> **What concepts need to be studied? What resources can help you be more effective? Invest in these.**

"How can I stay grounded?"

We can get so busy doing good that we lose ourselves in the process. Life can be so hectic that we forget who we are and why we do what we do. To stay grounded (and sane), we need to regularly ask five questions:

1) *Platform:* Who am I?

Can we answer this question without stating our title or role? If our identity is only in our jobs, we may be productive for a while, but our reserves of joy, hope, and love will gradually diminish.

2) *Priority:* What really matters?

If the answer is "everything," the real answer is "nothing." One of the hardest and most necessary tasks of leadership is to narrow the scope so our efforts have maximum impact. I've seen people write page after page of priorities as if the sheer volume demonstrates

VOICES: The Power, Pain, & Purpose of Voices

their commitment to excellence. It doesn't. Take time to think, pray, and talk to people who know you best and identify your top five priorities for the next year.

3) *Perspective:* Where am I going?

What stage of life are you in right now? What stage is your organization in? Look back to see the trajectory of your family life, finances, health, core leaders, and the impact of your church, nonprofit, or business. Gain perspective on where you've been, where you are, and where you're going.

4) *Purpose:* Why am I a leader?

What is your life's purpose? How do you know you're fulfilling it? Where are the holes at this point in your leadership? How will you fill them?

5) *People:* How do I define success?

This seems like an easy question, but it's not. We can read books, attend conferences, and hear podcasts about other leaders' stunning success, and we assume ours will be the same. It may, but it may not. Someday, we'll realize that our influence in the lives of a few people means more than anything.[28]

Questioning Voices

VOICES IN CRITICAL MOMENTS

Now, let's be more specific and address the voices we need to hear in critical moments as we lead.

"What do I think and feel, and how do I react, in times of stress?"

Momentary stress, like a package that arrives late or being stuck in traffic, doesn't raise our adrenaline levels very much, or if they do, it's only for a brief time. But prolonged, unrelieved stress occurs when the trend line of business sales or church attendance keeps going in the wrong direction, someone we love receives a tragic diagnosis, and we live under the weight of a painful situation day after day and week after week. In times like this, we need voices of understanding and support, and we also need expert voices to speak into the circumstances.

> In times like this, we need voices of understanding and support, and we also need expert voices to speak into the circumstances.

VOICES: The Power, Pain, & Purpose of Voices

"What do I think and feel, and how do I react, when people criticize me?"

Today's criticism has a way of attaching to yesterday's, so we feel the weight of the pebble and the boulder. First, we need to sort out what's true and helpful and what's not on target. Most of us initially react defensively, and many of us stay in that posture. That may be natural, but it's not constructive.

> **When our identity is threatened, we overreact; when our identity is secure, we can be calm and even welcome critiques of our talents and leadership.**

It often helps to have a sounding board, someone who can give us feedback and help us sort out the comments and our reactions. When our identity is threatened, we overreact; when our identity is secure, we can be calm and even welcome critiques of our talents and leadership.

Questioning Voices

"How do I respond to all the opportunities and challenges in the culture?"

I find myself in the middle of two different realities. Barna research shows that the trendlines aren't encouraging: In the church world, we've seen a persistent slide in attendance, volunteerism, giving, and other kinds of engagement. In our online society, connecting and disconnecting are so easy that when people feel the least bit uncomfortable, they look for something else.[29] But the churches where I consult and speak are living in a very different reality: attendance, giving, and the number of volunteers is at an all-time high. The two realities create very different challenges: one needs to find ways to attract and inspire more people; the other needs to harness the momentum for long-term impact.

In case you haven't noticed, there's another challenge facing all of us. If we thought our political climate would calm down, we've had a rude awakening. I know wonderful, godly people on all sides (and some who refuse to take sides), but too often, those in our churches believe their side has a monopoly on God's truth and love. They don't. We'll do much better in representing God's kingdom if we take the time to understand people who disagree with us. We may find that we want many of the same things, we just have different methods to get there. Jesus consistently stood for truth and grace, which confused some and infuriated others. If we follow Him, that'll be our experience too, at least to some extent.

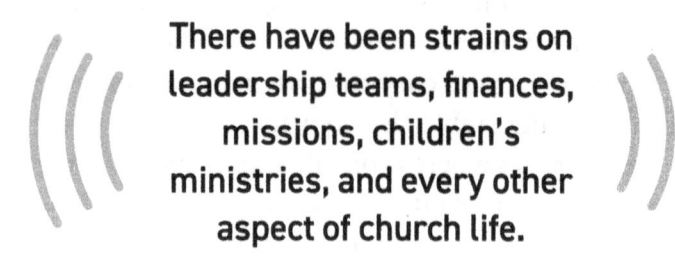

> **There have been strains on leadership teams, finances, missions, children's ministries, and every other aspect of church life.**

Recent global events forced us to rethink how we connect and communicate. Many of us learned to be wonderfully creative, and we thrived in the middle of uncertainty. But there have been strains on leadership teams, finances, missions, children's ministries, and every other aspect of church life.

In the middle of all this, we need to hear voices that consistently affirm our higher calling. We need to spend time with people who honor God, understand our challenges, respect the complexity of our situations, and remind us that Jesus is both Savior and Lord, the one true sacrifice and the one true King. We have a very difficult job of representing the God of grace in the middle of a divisive culture...and highly emotional people in our organizations.

"How can I handle conflict more effectively?"

This is a severe test of our leadership. When we feel threatened, part of our brains, the amygdala, instantly produces reactions to fight, flight, or freeze. You've seen all three in action: Some people "get big," they sit up or stand up, they lean forward, they get loud, and their faces shout, "You'd better watch out!" They're using intimidation to get their way and reduce their level of stress. Others look for the door! They can't get away fast enough. If they stay in the room, they hide behind a book or stare at a laptop. And still others are like a deer caught in the headlights—they can't think, they can't speak, and they can't move. When these three stress reactions happen in the amygdala, the pre-frontal cortex (the thinking part of the brain) shuts down, so all that's left is our instantaneous and overwhelming reaction.

This is a severe test of our leadership.

VOICES: The Power, Pain, & Purpose of Voices

Debbie Goldstein is a lecturer at Harvard Law School and the managing partner of Triad Consulting Group, which specializes in leadership development. She says that when conversations get tough, good leaders become curious. Instead of reacting in self-protective ways (fight, flight, or freeze), they ask, "What are you thinking but not saying?" This question cuts through surface issues to get to the heart of the matter, and the dialogue that comes from it builds trust and enables two people to look for a workable solution.

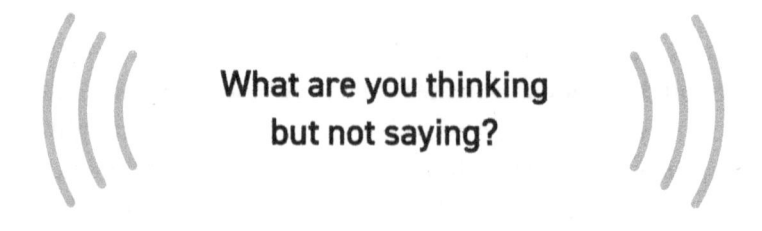

What are you thinking but not saying?

Goldstein and her team of researchers found that problem-solving in conflict often quickly turns into blaming and defending... which only creates another problem in the relationship. Normally, our instinctive question is, "Who's right?" And our immediate conclusion is, "Me!" Of course, the corollary question is, "Who's wrong?" With the conclusion, "Anyone but me!" We then follow up with accusatory questions, such as, "What's wrong with you?" "Why did you do that?" Goldstein observes, "There's zero chance that it's going to go well." Instead, she recommends a different set of questions, such as, "How did each of us contribute to the problem?" "What's a workable solution?" To lower the temperature and invite open conversation, we need to let go of our certainty that we're always right and move toward open-minded curiosity about the cause and solution to the problem. She recommends three steps:

1) Objectively assess the problem.

This may not be as easy as it sounds. From the beginning, many people want to point the finger away from themselves. They want to minimize their involvement and maximize anyone else's. It's best to wait to begin the assessment until after emotions have cooled, at least from white-hot to simmering.

Then, ask the right people to join you to analyze what happened. Who are the right people? Generally, it's those who have participated in the planning and execution, but it may be wise to have a smaller group, or perhaps invite a mentor or coach to facilitate the conversation. Begin with a history of how the decision was made, the planning process, the delegation of responsibility, oversight, and execution. Avoid

VOICES: The Power, Pain, & Purpose of Voices

assigning blame. Stick to the facts and keep calm no matter how others react.

At the end of the assessment, you and the others involved should have a clear idea of what happened and why it happened.

> Avoid assigning blame. Stick to the facts, and keep calm no matter how others react.

2) Be aware of your own subtext.

In every conversation, there's a text and a subtext. The words we say are the text, and the hidden motivations are the subtext. When leaders are less than secure, their subtext might be, "Please tell me I'm okay!", "I can't let anyone think I'm wrong!" or "I'm in charge here. Don't cross me!" The question is: What's going on under the surface that shapes how we listen, think, and speak?

3) Be curious, not condemning.

This is when you should ask the person, "What are you thinking that you're not saying?"

Instead of rushing to judgment to assign blame, open the dialogue to explore the person's inner world. Read body language and notice the tone of voice but go further than receiving information about the person. Be curious. Goldstein explains that we may notice a gap between what the person is saying and what they're thinking. For instance, a normally quiet person may look very angry and about to explode, or a talkative person may give clipped, one-word answers to open-ended questions. Asking what they're thinking invites open, honest conversation. She observes,

> *It's a demonstration that you really care. People won't always respond, but I'm shocked at how often you will get a candid answer. Because it's a demonstration that you're noticing them, that you care what they think, and that you want to have a real conversation.*[30]

Go further than receiving information about the person. Be curious.

VOICES: The Power, Pain, & Purpose of Voices

VOICING QUESTIONS DURING SEASONS OF GROWTH

Growth is a wonderful thing, but it inevitably raises questions for leaders. People's perceptions of their leaders tend to be stuck at the point when either they or you entered the organization. For example, when I became the president of a Bible college, we had eighty-seven students; when I left, we were fully accredited with an enrollment of over 800. But those who were there at the beginning still saw me as "the new guy." They expected me to be just as available as I had been when we could fit everybody in a small room.

The expectations of people aren't sterile and academic; they're emotional and visceral. Jesus came to rescue the world from sin and death (which is a pretty broad vision!), and along the way, he built strong relationships with people. The Gospels give us a glimpse into His close connections with three siblings: Mary, Martha, and Lazarus. When Jesus was far from their home in Bethany, Lazarus got very sick. The sisters had seen Him heal others, "So they sent word to Jesus, 'Lord, the one you love is sick'" (John 11:3). This was a voice crying out with deep emotion. Surely he wouldn't refuse a plea like that! But Jesus had a higher agenda, one that confused and deeply hurt the sisters. He waited until Lazarus had died, and then He arrived in

Bethany. He first encountered Martha, who, it seems to me, had a bit of an edge in her voice as she told him, "Lord . . . if you had been here, my brother would not have died" (John 11:21). Then someone told Mary Jesus had come. Her words were the same as her sister's: "Lord, if you had been here, my brother would not have died" (John 11:32).

> **The expectations of people aren't sterile and academic; they're emotional and visceral.**

Jesus' ministry had grown, but the sisters expected Him to be available like He had been before. They were disappointed and hurt when He didn't come when they wanted Him to. It's the same for church leaders when their ministries expand. They're not as available, but the people who have been there when the church was small still assume they'll drop what they're doing to respond immediately. When the leaders don't, their pleas become more emotional, and some simply can't handle the change in the leader's expanding role.

VOICES: The Power, Pain, & Purpose of Voices

> **If you want these questions to stimulate open communication, create an atmosphere conducive to making people feel safe when they feel a bit vulnerable.**

As your organization grows...
- » How will your priorities become more focused?
- » Since you can't be available to everyone, who will get your attention?
- » How will you staff for future growth?
- » How will you identify the multipliers?
- » Will you be comfortable with gifted staff members receiving praise?

VOICING QUESTIONS FOR YOUR LEADERS

It's wise to model the voice of asking great questions by posing them to your staff team and key volunteers. Many of these are similar to the ones you ask yourself, including:

- » What negative voice are you giving too much space in your head?
- » What voices speak life into you?

Questioning Voices

- » What are the most productive aspects of your role?
- » What are you doing to accelerate your leadership skills?
- » What are some ways you can handle stress more effectively?
- » And criticism?
- » And conflict?
- » What are two or three things you'd like us to change?
- » What two or three things do we need to keep and do even better?
- » What resources do you need that aren't presently available?
- » When and where do you feel heard?
- » Do you feel valued? What can I do to show my appreciation for you?

If you want these questions to stimulate open communication, create an atmosphere conducive to making people feel safe when they feel a bit vulnerable. You might meet with people one-on-one or in small groups. When people share, notice the nonverbal communication as well as the words, and if you sense any tension, ask the question, "What are you thinking that you're not saying?"

VOICES: The Power, Pain, & Purpose of Voices

Some people may feel reluctant to be candid in these conversations. Your goal isn't to force the issue but to affirm, accept, and open the door to further discussions.

VOICING QUESTIONS FOR YOUR ORGANIZATION

Leaders know that change is a constant in every growing organization. Great leaders lead change, good leaders respond to change, and poor leaders resist change. Of course, some forms of change aren't desirable, so leaders need wisdom to discern where a particular change falls on the continuum from welcome to unwelcome.

Primary Questions

In the first chapter of my book, *Change Has Changed*, I explained the need for leaders to think critically about their organizations:

> *It's easy to feel overwhelmed by the avalanche of news, which is mostly bad news and warnings that things will get even worse! If we're not careful, we'll either become reactive without thinking (which causes our people to doubt our wisdom) or we'll become passive and sullen (which invites them to look somewhere else for direction). In*

Questioning Voices

times of uncertainty, leaders need to ask five crucial questions:

1) What should we START?
For some, it's inconceivable to make plans to start something new as they cope with tragedy and loss, but great leaders know that down times (in the market and the community) offer incredible opportunities to those who are wise and nimble.

2) What should we STOP?
We realize that at least some of the meetings, programs, and events we planned in "normal" times don't fit any longer. We'll be wasting our time and resources if we insist on continuing them.

3) What should we SUSPEND until later?
Some activities will be appropriate later, but not now. We need to triage our plans to focus on those that will make the biggest difference in the short term.

4) What needs to be SUSTAINED at all costs?
Organizational values cannot be sacrificed in any way. The *what, how,* and *when* may change, but the *purpose and values* remain the organization's guiding light.

VOICES: The Power, Pain, & Purpose of Voices

5) What will accelerate our SPEED of growth?

In a sustained crisis, people in the community and potential customers are looking for organizations that can adapt to the changing environment, speak to their emotional needs as well as their physical needs, and offer services and products they desperately want. The churches and businesses that see these opportunities will grow ... and the others will falter and perhaps die.

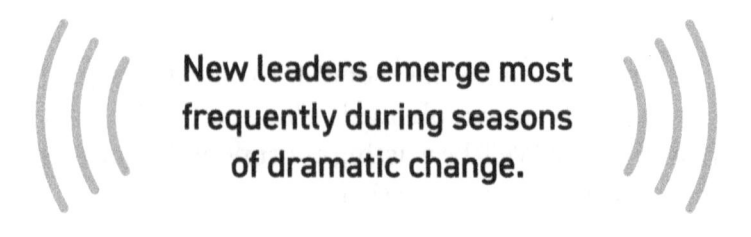

> **New leaders emerge most frequently during seasons of dramatic change.**

These are important questions when things are going well ... they're crucial when we face times of uncertainty, strain, and doubt.

The Question of Raising Up New Leaders

Every growing organization finds ways to identify, challenge, enlist, train, place, and oversee new leaders. New leaders emerge most frequently during seasons of dramatic change—either from exponential growth

Questioning Voices

because they want to get on the train with us, or in a crisis when they step up to help solve the problem. For leaders, these two seasons can consume our attention and energy so we don't observe who is stepping up.

As leaders, we are so busy triaging problems and handling challenges that our peripheral vision is sometimes limited, so we don't notice rising leaders. We must be intentional.

The Question of Messaging

Communication is crucial—and more difficult—as an organization grows. When a church is small, it's easy to connect with everyone, often on a first-name basis. But as the church hits targets of 200, 400, and more, personal connections are far harder to make. How can leaders communicate effectively with everyone throughout the church? By cascading their message. How does that work? I'm glad you asked. First, the pastor and staff team need to craft the message (about a new building, new program, new emphasis, or whatever God has put on their hearts). When the staff team has been bought in, the pastor shares the plan with the board and/or top-level leaders, or in reverse order given that context. They then become conduits of the message to the next level of leaders, perhaps small group leaders. The pastor leads the meeting, and the

VOICES: The Power, Pain, & Purpose of Voices

other leaders share their excitement about the possibilities. When these people grasp the vision, the pastor then communicates the concept to the church, with some top leaders and second-level leaders sharing their passion for it too. In this way, people throughout the church realize the vision isn't just the pastor's idea; the leaders of the church are behind it.

In the business world, messaging is crucial. In an article in *Inc.*, Martin Zwilling, founder and CEO of Startup Professionals, says that business leaders must develop better communication skills to relate inside and outside their companies. He recommends:

Influence and collaboration trump command and control. No longer can leaders consider communication as "information out, information in." You can't hide behind your technical expertise or a formally appointed role. To be a leader with influence, you must create a culture of engagement and participation, through your language in all channels. [And...]

Communication must address content and relationship. Every act of communication now has two messages: a content message and a relationship message. The content is what you want to say, and the other half is how you express your attitudes and feelings. Either can get you valued and followed, or rejected by your team and your customers.[31]

Some leaders instinctively blend information and inspiration, but no one has an excuse to remain stagnant. All of us can learn to connect more effectively to people on our teams, our vendors, customers, and the public.

The Question of Decision-Making
Organizational growth requires us to acquire (or refine) skills of decision-making. A study by Bain & Company found that an organization's decision effectiveness has a 95 percent correlation with future success. The researchers found, "While nearly everyone would accept the premise about the connection between decisions and results... few companies look systematically at what gets in the way of good decision making and execution. And few take the actions necessary to improve how they make and execute their important decisions."[32]

One of the most important roles of leaders of growing organizations is determining who is part of the decision-making process. In the past, probably only a few participated, but with growth, we want to be sure leaders throughout the organization feel

VOICES: The Power, Pain, & Purpose of Voices

heard and own the decisions, so at least some decisions are pushed down to the granular level. This means the senior leader and other top leaders must be clear about the vision and strategy while leaving some of the details of implementation to team leaders. This can be tricky. Perfectionist leaders want to control every decision, so they don't let others get involved. But if leaders don't give clear direction, letting others make decisions can lead to chaos—that is, unnecessary chaos.

> **One of the most important roles of leaders of growing organizations is determining who is part of the decision-making process.**

Growth requires periodic assessments of organizational structures. I've found it helpful to ask the simple question: "Who does what by when?"
- » Delegation: Who is responsible?
- » Responsibility: What are the goals, the resources, and the processes?

Questioning Voices

» Timing: Decisions are often made in meetings and executed by teams. Coordination is crucial, so deadlines and clear communication among teams are more important than ever.

The Question of Staffing

As I mentioned in Chapter 4, in every kind of organization, leaders often put up with poorly performing staff members far longer than we should. We want to give them the benefit of the doubt, but we do them no favors by letting them persist in dragging the team's culture down. Yes, we need to be kind and understanding, and we need to give people opportunities to improve, but at some point, our calling to expand the kingdom requires us to make some hard decisions. So, the first two staffing questions are:

1) Who needs some kind of standard of performance review?
2) Who has had ample opportunities to change but hasn't shown enough improvement?

A productive exercise for any leader is to step back from the normal delegation and reporting structure and ask, "If I had a blank organizational chart, who would I put in charge of what responsibilities, and why would I make those decisions?" You might find that some changes jump out at you.

VOICES: The Power, Pain, & Purpose of Voices

We've all heard the old saying, "If you want something done, give it to a busy person." There's some truth to that, but another truth is that the new responsibility either has to be added to an already crammed schedule or at least some existing responsibilities won't receive the same level of attention. Another way to handle this is to match the talented staff member to a new assignment and tell the team, "I've asked Bill to be in charge of this project for the next month. He's devoting 100 percent of his time and energy to the project. If he needs your help, give him your full cooperation. This means he won't be doing his regular responsibilities. He's delegating this part to Jan, that part to Phil, and another to Alisha. If you have questions or if you need to coordinate on events or projects, work with them." Bill's monthlong assignment could be anything the leader needs at this point in the growth of the organization: streamlining processes, exploring new products, changing the reporting structure, launching new projects, opening new venues, etc. This means, of course, the leader has to do a cost/benefit analysis before giving Bill the novel role. There will be challenges for Jan, Phil, Alisha, and others on the team while Bill is focused on the new role, but the benefits may prove to be well worth the temporary inconvenience. If it works, the leader may use this approach for other projects and, perhaps, for other staff members. When I was president at the university, I actually had such a person. I called him my "zero to ten miles per hour" person. He got an envisioned project started, got it to "10" and handed it off to someone he had mentored in the process. When I consult with organizations, I call this person CSO (Chief Strategic Officer). Your organization might be ready for such a person on your organizational chart.

> **If you're spending a lot of time soothing hurt feelings and trying to get your team to collaborate even at a minimal level, you may have some wrong people on your team.**

Some leaders feel threatened by others getting attention and applause (that was Saul's problem with David's acclaim after killing Goliath), but great leaders hire people who have exemplary talents ... and these leaders lead the celebration of their staff members'

VOICES: The Power, Pain, & Purpose of Voices

success. Gifted people bring energy as well as talent to the team. They stimulate creativity and bring out the best in others. People who bring expertise invariably have ideas that can shake up the system and identify ways to have a greater impact.

If you're spending a lot of time soothing hurt feelings and trying to get your team to collaborate even at a minimal level, you may have some wrong people on your team.

- » How well is your team functioning?
- » With a blank organizational chart, where would you put people?
- » How might a monthlong targeted assignment for a particularly gifted staff member move your church forward?
- » Is there a lid on the level of talent you want on the team?

Every organization experiences ebbs and flows, times of growth, and times when leaders have to recharge for the next season of growth. Change isn't the enemy, but leaders need to ask the right questions to the right people at the right times so change moves the organization forward.

Questions are important voices. They make people think more deeply, uncover hidden opportunities, and

Questioning Voices

shake up the system. Learn to ask great questions, and then acquire the habit of asking second and third questions to probe a bit more. And with each one, listen... really listen. People will feel understood, you'll build trust, and your organization will thrive.

> **Questions are important voices.
> Learn to ask great questions.**

THINK ABOUT IT:

1) Take some time to ask yourself the questions in the first part of this chapter.

2) What are two or three major applications from this reflection?

3) When, where, and how often do you want to pose questions to your leaders?

4) What difference will it make?

VOICES: The Power, Pain, & Purpose of Voices

5) Which of the questions about organizations are most important for you to ask at this point?

6) Where do you expect pushback?

7) What are some ways to bring people (your team, top lay leaders, and the whole organization) along?

THE VOICE IN YOUR HEAD BECOMES THE VOICE IN YOUR MOUTH. THE VOICE IN YOUR MOUTH BECOMES THE VOICE IN OTHERS' HEADS.

CHAPTER 9

Tailoring Your Voice

WHERE IS YOUR ORGANIZATION IN THE GROWTH CYCLE? Are you meeting and exceeding your goals? Are your leaders aware of your successes? Or do you sense that your momentum is slowing down? Is your leadership pipeline turning out plenty of eager, competent new leaders? It's crucial to tailor your voice of vision to meet the needs of the moment—and sometimes, those needs aren't evident yet.

The familiar "S-curve" is used by CEOs and project managers to create a graph to represent predictable

VOICES: The Power, Pain, & Purpose of Voices

phases in the life cycle of a business or project. Leaders use this model to give them a clear voice of vision, direction, and warning. Typically, organizations of all kinds follow this pattern:

Organizations often start slowly at first and then have a burst of growth when the combination of vision, resources, and proven success accelerates growth. Sooner or later, the project moves toward completion or exhaustion, loss of vision, or some other factor causes a plateau, and if it's not arrested, the growth curve moves downward. The voices we hear (and say) at each phase might sound like this:

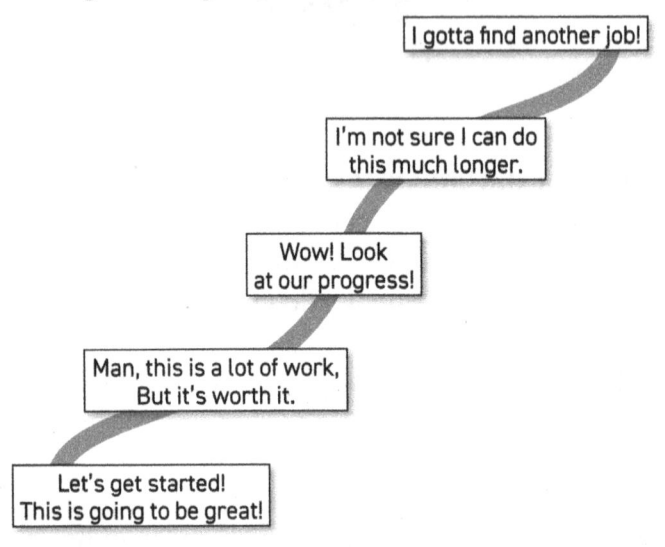

> I gotta find another job!

> I'm not sure I can do this much longer.

> Wow! Look at our progress!

> Man, this is a lot of work, But it's worth it.

> Let's get started! This is going to be great!

Tailoring Your Voice

In a *Forbes* article, Anna Baluch explains,
Project managers often use an S-curve to track the progress of a project and pinpoint potential issues. An S-curve can also help them compare the actual progress of a project to the planned progress so they understand performance and whether or not any changes need to be made.

Before a project starts, most project managers create a schedule that outlines the required resources and sequence of work. This schedule is known as the baseline schedule and the S-curve that comes from it is known as the baseline S-curve. The baseline S-curve shows the expected progress of a project.[33]

> **The infusion of a fresh voice of vision before the plateau is necessary for the organization to continue to grow.**

However, if a leader anticipates the need in an ongoing project (like leading a business or a church) to change before momentum wanes, and he institutes growth strategies, two things happen: The organization can overcome the tendency to plateau and decline, and many people will be confused and resistant. The infusion of a fresh voice of vision before the plateau is necessary for the organization to continue to grow.

RHYTHMS OF CHANGE

Outstanding leaders understand that people respond to change in various ways, from eager acceptance to fierce resistance, so it's crucial to create "a rhythm of change." Dominic Barton, former global managing partner of McKinsey, observed that the leader's voice at those critical moments is like attaching a defibrillator to the organization to shock it back to life.[34] The rhythm, with the defibrillator attached, looks like this:

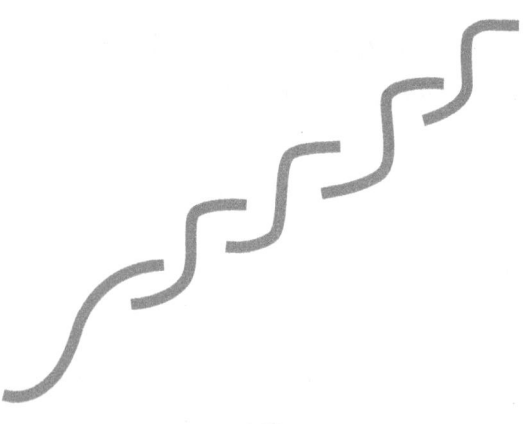

Tailoring Your Voice

This uncomfortable time can be avoided, but only if the leader takes the necessary steps to inject vision and energy into the organization at the point when momentum is slipping. In other words, wise leaders do what's necessary for continued growth when few others see the need for change.

> **Wise leaders do what's necessary for continued growth when few others see the need for change.**

When I became the president of Beulah Heights Bible College, I started with a divinely inspired vision, but we had quite a hill to climb. The first cycle of the S-curve had slow growth, but innovative ideas, tons of energy, and a big investment in relational capital got us going in the right direction. Our numerical growth, and all that brings in hiring professors and staff members and providing more resources for students, began to level off. To grow, we had to get accredited. It took time, effort, and a forest full of paper for applications,

VOICES: The Power, Pain, & Purpose of Voices

but when we were finally accredited, our growth took off again. This was the second S-curve. After a few years of sustained growth, our momentum slowed again. This time, we had to address the excellence of our staff. We went through a painful but necessary reorganization, which gave us a new vision for even greater numbers. This was another S-curve. I didn't have the language of the S-curve at the time, but I intuitively sensed when it was necessary to inject new energy into the system so we could grow again. When I look back, I can see the rhythm very clearly. We actually went through eight separate phases of the S-curve during my tenure at the college.

> Your voice—when you see the need for change but others don't—needs to be calm and confident.

Your voice—when you see the need for change but others don't—needs to be calm and confident. To be sure, some people will see the need too, and they'll be on board from the beginning; most people will need time to process the confusion of making changes while things are going well, but they'll come around; and a few will be resistant to the end. Don't let the doubters dominate your message! Cast vision, communicate the reasons for change and instill hope in those who listen.

It's not just that *they're* resistant to change—*we're* often resistant. We have a track record, we have chosen our team, we've crafted the plan...all of which makes it harder to say, "Hey, we need to do something different!" A business executive commented, "The problem with being a CEO a long time is everybody tells you that you have all the answers. It's comforting to your ego but very dangerous."[35]

THE VOICE OF COLLABORATION

In his book *Thinking, Fast and Slow*, Nobel-prize-winning economist Daniel Kahneman describes one of his experiments that shows the impact of buy-in. One group was randomly assigned numbered lottery tickets, and the same number of people was given tickets and a pen for them to choose their numbers. Before the drawing, Kahneman and his team offered to buy back tickets from those in both groups. They expected the number who accepted their offer would be the same because the lottery is based on pure chance, but in repeated experiments with people from different ethnic groups or socio-economic status, and the size of the lottery prize, those who wrote down their number demanded five times more than the ones who were assigned random numbers. Kahneman concluded this response is "predictably irrational."[36] It's *predictable* because people who have invested something expect more, but it's *irrational* because there's no greater inherent value in any particular ticket. People take ownership of what they help create.

> The crusader approach may work well in combat or in a crisis, but it doesn't build trust or make people feel valued.

In an article in *Harvard Business Review*, the authors contrast two distinct leadership styles: the crusader and the collaborative leader. Crusaders dominate conversations, insist on their point of view, communicate with intensity and passion, interrupt others, and are visibly frustrated by any resistance, assuming other people don't know what they're talking about.

The crusader approach may work well in combat or in a crisis, but it doesn't build trust or make people feel valued. The authors explain,

A more effective approach to driving change in the workplace involves adopting the mindset of a collaborator. Instead of doggedly pursuing a myopic perspective, collaborators focus on building relationships, understanding organizational dynamics and reasons for resistance, and using this knowledge to advocate for change in a shared, strategic manner.

Collaborative leaders invite differing points of view, are patient with the process of discovery, build relationships of trust, and treat people with respect. The authors conclude,

The need for change is inevitable in any organization, but the approach to driving change is a determinant of its success or failure.... Affecting lasting change is not a solitary quest, but an inherently shared effort. It requires embracing a collaborative mindset that respects and includes diverse perspectives, maintains a strategic focus, and patiently navigates the complexities of

VOICES: The Power, Pain, & Purpose of Voices

organizational dynamics. It's not about surrendering your passion or advocacy but leveraging them in a more inclusive, strategic, and ultimately effective way.[37]

Some of us were taught and mentored by crusader leaders, so that style is ingrained in us. But we'll be more effective if we involve people in the decision-making process. Take steps to make collaboration the norm, and involve more people in decision-making. If you're losing momentum in your current S-curve, changing your leadership style may be a good starting point. There are many workable styles, but what's needed at this crucial juncture are shifts:

- » from control to collaboration,
- » from answers to questions,
- » from large groups to small groups,
- » or maybe from small groups to large groups, and
- » from making assumptions to clear communication.

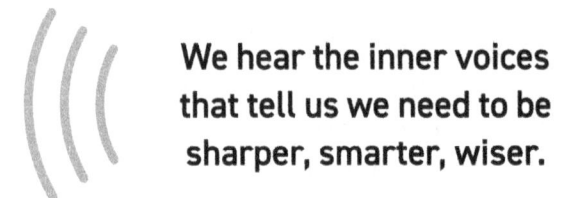

> We hear the inner voices that tell us we need to be sharper, smarter, wiser.

Tailoring Your Voice

LISTENING AND LEARNING

Leaders are learners. A sharp, clear, challenging vision stretches us to be our best, which means we need to expose ourselves to all kinds of resources. We hear the inner voices that tell us we need to be sharper, smarter, wiser. We want to be ready for every opportunity and every challenge that comes our way. We read great books, we listen to amazing speakers, and we spend time with people who sharpen our thinking. When we plan for the next board meeting, staff meeting, or interaction with a big donor, we want to be smarter than we were last time. But we also need to keep our ears to the ground.

In the early years of a church's, a nonprofit's, or a business's existence, leaders were involved at the ground level, talking to visitors or customers, board members, and anyone else who walked through the doors. With growth came requests to join organizations, speak at events, and enjoy acclaim... all of which can become a distraction to the job of leading with wisdom and courage in the next period of change and uncertainty. Great leaders stay connected to the grassroots while keeping their vision on the next season of growth. Ed Breen, CEO of Dupont, stays sharp by spending time brainstorming with other CEOs: "I engage with activists. If you listen, they often have

VOICES: The Power, Pain, & Purpose of Voices

good ideas. . . . I still meet with groups like this now. I always walk away with six or seven new ideas."[38] Similarly, Intuit CEO Brad Smith shadows leaders of other tech giants once a quarter, watching, listening, and jotting down his observations. But Smith also learns from people at all levels of the org chart at his company. He schedules two meetings a week with people at all levels of Intuit, with eight to ten in each group. He asks them three questions:

1) "What's getting better than it was six months ago?"
2) "What's not making enough progress or going in the wrong direction?" and
3) "What's something you're afraid no one is telling me that you believe I need to know?"

> **In my consulting experience with organizations across the world, I've seen that many leaders assume that all wisdom resides in the executive suite. It doesn't. Real wisdom resides in the grassroots.**

Tailoring Your Voice

These meetings proved incredibly valuable because input wasn't filtered by managers.[39]

It's important for leaders to go far beyond the staff team and the board when asking these questions. Top leaders can be insulated and isolated, and many people tell them only what they think the leaders want to hear. Who has grassroots insights? In churches, who has their finger on the pulse of the people? The parking lot attendants, greeters, ushers, small group leaders, and all the others who regularly hear the voices of those the top leaders may not normally hear. In nonprofits, the volunteers and frontline workers see the nitty gritty of the organization's effectiveness. And in business, smart execs find time to talk with people far down the organizational chart. Years ago before technology enabled accurate readings of the air quality in mines, canaries were carried into the heart of the earth. If the air was good enough, the canaries kept singing; if it wasn't, the canaries died. It was the miners' early warning system. Our early warning system is taking plenty of time to hear the voices of people at every level of the organization ... including visitors, volunteers, call center employees, and customers.

In my consulting experience with organizations across the world, I've seen that many leaders assume that all wisdom resides in the executive suite. It doesn't. Real wisdom resides in the grassroots. If I want to discover what's really going on in an organization, I make a point to hear the voices of the janitor, the receptionist, the greeters, and the frontline volunteers. They have their eyes and ears wide open, and they can tell me what's really happening. I've also noticed that quite often their observations aren't valued, so their observations can easily turn into complaints, which then causes the top leaders to ignore them completely. When that happens, the canaries stop singing.

AVOID ANCHORING

When senior leaders have been leading for a long time, they intuitively make assumptions based on past successes and failures. This is called "anchoring," which is the brain's way of simplifying complex decisions. Many leaders plan for the upcoming year by looking only at past experience, existing team members, and current programs, but wise leaders step back and look at their teams and their churches with a consultant's eyes. This is what it might look like.

Four decades ago, Intel's profits dropped from $198 million to $2 million in one year. The president, Andy Grove, asked the CEO, Gordon Moore, what would happen if he and his management team were fired by the board and a new CEO and team were installed.

Tailoring Your Voice

Moore answered that a new leader would radically change the nature of the company by replacing their primary product with an upgrade. Grove asked him, "Why shouldn't you and I walk out the door, come back, and do it ourselves?" Which is exactly what they did. They switched to the production of microprocessors, which was the source of tremendous growth for decades.[40]

> **If you were invited to be a consultant in your organization, what questions would you ask the leaders?**

If you were invited to be a consultant in your organization, what questions would you ask the leaders? What advantages would you identify? What hindrances would you need to address? What would be your recommendations? A consultant's voice could bring new light to their situation, stimulate creativity, and propel them forward.

VOICES: The Power, Pain, & Purpose of Voices

What if you took on a consultant's role at your organization?

> You'll sense the need for change before you see it.

THE PIVOT

A fresh vision, though, is only part of the solution to avoid a downward trajectory on the S-curve. You'll sense the need for change before you see it. At that moment, it's vital to involve people in the planning process. In *Good to Great*, Jim Collins explained that some boards are looking for a hero to come in and lead their organizations, and they act like "a genius with a thousand helpers." Collins' research showed that the most successful companies don't have leaders like that. Instead, their CEOs and presidents are collaborative, bringing out the best in people on their teams, listening to their creative ideas, and celebrating their skills and success.[41] This doesn't mean the leader is passive. At the pivotal moment, the leader has to be bold in laying out the vision for change, answer a lot of reasonable

Tailoring Your Voice

questions, and not let opposition derail him. When there's sufficient buy-in, it's wise to involve team members in the planning to unleash their potential.

Organizational growth requires adjustments. The schedule, relationships, and priorities you had when your organization was small can't take you where your vision wants to go. When the defibrillator is attached, you'll need to:

1) Rewrite your job responsibilities.

Before, you did everything—preaching, counseling, administration, teaching, weddings, funerals, hospital visits, discipleship, and answering calls in the middle of the night—because no one else could. But as your church grows, you need to focus on doing fewer things exceptionally well and delegate the rest to competent, trained, and resourced people on your team. The same pattern is often true in nonprofits and businesses.

2) Focus on leadership development.

If the number of people your organization touches is like a pile of sand, it can only grow by broadening the base. If you pour more sand on a narrow base, it falls off the edge. To shift metaphors, you want to have a wide funnel to attract as many people as possible to your organization, and as they get more involved, be more intentional in selection, training, placing, and

VOICES: The Power, Pain, & Purpose of Voices

overseeing emergent leaders. The real measure of success is the quality and quantity of leaders throughout the organization.

3) Invest in more effective systems.

Yes, I know. You're a gifted speaker, and you've seen remarkable growth because people love to hear you preach, or in business, you may be incredibly gifted in startups, but there's a ceiling on growth if you don't create efficient management structures. This may not *be* your thing, but it has to *become* your thing. I'm not advocating bureaucracy that takes on a life of its own, becomes a beast you and your leaders have to feed, and sucks the life out of you. Good systems maximize creativity, innovative solutions, time management, and overall effectiveness. They free each person to function at their highest level.

4) Say "NO" to more requests and demands.

Investment expert Warren Buffett remarked, "The difference between successful people and really successful people is that really successful people say 'no' to almost everything."[42] When you were struggling to get traction, you were almost invisible to other leaders, but success brings attention and opportunities . . . sometimes too much attention and too many opportunities. Most of the outstanding leaders I know experienced a season when they spoke at too many events and had less energy for their churches. But they learned they didn't have to agree to be everything to everyone. Success also brings people out of the woodwork with ideas to improve what you're doing—they have a new strategy, a new resource, a new method, or something else you "really have to" implement. Lean toward "no" until you're thoroughly convinced an idea might be a "maybe."

5) Be prepared for pushback.

I've known leaders who were great friends until one of them experienced remarkable growth. Then the other one became distant . . . questioned the successful leader's motives, and even worse, questioned his motives to some of their peers. You would think everyone would celebrate success—and plenty of people do, but a few compare and feel threatened. They complain (at least internally), *It's not fair! I'm as gifted and smart. Why isn't my organization growing like that? There must be some nefarious reason.* Their criticism is more a reflection of their insecurity than anything you've done. Forgive them, love them, and pray for them.[43]

VOICES: The Power, Pain, & Purpose of Voices

FUTURE-PROOFING

When things are going well, it's hard to imagine a crisis just over the horizon.

I'm not referring to a pandemic, an economic collapse, or a natural disaster. I'm talking about complacency. Some college and professional coaches won championships but were fired only a few years later. In fact, ten NFL coaches whose teams won the Super Bowl were fired when their teams couldn't sustain success.[44]

> I'm talking about complacency.

Boeing CEO Dennis Muilenburg was named *Aviation Week*'s Person of the Year in 2018, but eleven months later, the board asked him to step down when two 737 MAX planes fell from the sky killing hundreds of people. British Petroleum's Tony Hayward was at the pinnacle of his career until the Deepwater Horizon offshore oil platform exploded and sank, spilling thousands of barrels of crude oil into the Gulf of Mexico. When the spill couldn't be contained quickly, he was forced to resign. A sudden crisis like these two

Tailoring Your Voice

examples can derail a leader's plans, but we create our own crises by not anticipating the need to change. When that happens, people aren't looking at outside forces to blame... they're looking at you.

We could list a number of high-profile pastors and business leaders who, for different reasons, are no longer leading their organizations. We need to prepare for both kinds of crises—those from outside causes and those that are self-inflicted. From time to time (at least once a year), it's smart to ask your board and team, "How would we prepare for the next crisis—a worldwide virus outbreak, an economic collapse, or our building burned to the ground?" Netflix CEO Reed Hastings poses a problem to his team, "It's ten years out, and Netflix is a failed firm. Estimate the probabilities of the different causes." Sometimes the team's conversation comes up with clear threats and practical solutions, "but many times, just defining what risks we face will prompt people to adjust behavior in smart ways that make us more resilient."[45] This conversation might seem irrelevant for your team and your church... until it isn't. It's also prudent to ask, "What are we doing—or not doing—that could lead to severe problems?" You might identify unresolved conflict between team or board members, exhaustion

VOICES: The Power, Pain, & Purpose of Voices

in you and others on the team, or a gradual slide toward irrelevance in the community.

> **The quality of relationships is tested in a crisis.**

Future-proofing your organization involves an array of contingency plans: What do we do if...? What do we do when...? You'll need a plan for what leaders need to know and do, plans for different types of crises, and effective communication platforms. In any kind of crisis, people feel vulnerable, so one of the main jobs of a leader is to reassure people that a plan is in place and the plan is workable. The quality of relationships is tested in a crisis. Those that were shaky crumble into dissension; those that were strong become even stronger. In difficult times, people can tell if we truly care for them, and they'll never forget how we treated them—either with love and support...or not. If we've built strong relationships based on mutual trust, when the worst happens, people will consider us innocent until proven guilty...instead of the other way around. Good will pays big dividends.

I experienced the benefits of trust not long ago. The email account of one of my clients was hacked, and his office received an email, purportedly from me, saying they were behind on payments and they needed to pay their invoice. The pastor's wife emailed me and wrote, "Sam, I'm so sorry we're late. We'll get this to you right away. Our church's CFO died yesterday of a heart attack. He and his family had no idea he had heart trouble. We're still in shock, but we'll take care of it right away."

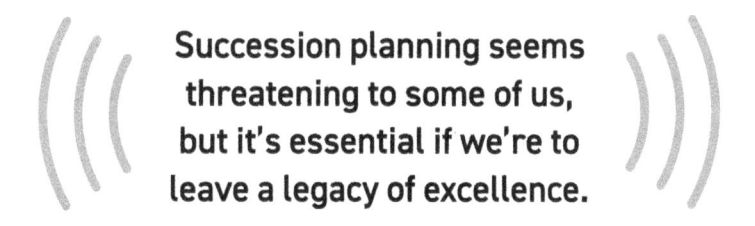

> Succession planning seems threatening to some of us, but it's essential if we're to leave a legacy of excellence.

I was confused. I hadn't sent a late notice to them. I was very sorry to hear about the staff member's sudden death, and I wanted to make sure the pastor's wife understood that the email wasn't from me. Actually,

VOICES: The Power, Pain, & Purpose of Voices

the AI program that hacked their account read about the man's death and sent them a condolence email!

When I explained that I hadn't sent the late notice, she told me, "When we got this email, my husband and I looked at each other. He said, 'This doesn't sound like Sam Chand.'" Because we respect and trust each other, they gave me the benefit of the doubt.

Future-proofing is an investment in new leaders. If we wait to coach rising leaders until the crisis hits, it's too late. Implement a coaching strategy now and reap the benefits in the good times and the hard ones. This also involves a replacement for you. Succession planning seems threatening to some of us, but it's essential if we're to leave a legacy of excellence. Well before you plan to retire, have conversations with your board. Put a plan in place, even if it has a lot of uncertainties at this point. As you get closer to retirement (or perhaps repositioning in the church or leaving), plans can be updated, clarified, and put into motion.

At every stage of our tenure as leaders, we need to future-proof our well-being. When we shoulder too much of the burden or experience conflict or other kinds of stress, our spirits feel weighed down. We can also struggle emotionally, physically, spiritually, and relationally. Burnout isn't a sign of zealous commitment; it's a sign we have misplaced priorities.

Tailoring Your Voice

THE VOICE OF HOPE

You have a high privilege and an enormous responsibility to be the voice of hope for your people. The first time you hook up the defibrillator will almost certainly feel daunting. At times, you may be as confused as those who follow you! But when you get through the first cycle, you'll gain a lot of savvy and confidence. Then, a few years after the first reboot when you dodged the downturn and led your organization to new heights, a plateau will lurk in the shadows of your future. But this time, you'll know what to do. No, your plan and strategy won't be exactly what they were the first time, but you'll ask the analytical questions, you'll be your own consultant, you'll get input from others who have been down this road, and you'll chart a new path through the next phase of change. And then you'll do it again and again and again, Lord willing that you'll be in your role that long.

We have strengths. Our routines and patterns have worked well for us. We have a vision that has sustained us and our organizations, but change is inevitable. We need to tailor our voice to fit the needs of the moment and one that reaches into the future. First, of course, we need to recognize that change is shifting the sand beneath our feet, and we need to be aware of it. Our voice in the past has been clear and strong, but it may

VOICES: The Power, Pain, & Purpose of Voices

need some adjustments so we and our churches can thrive in the future.

It doesn't work, though, to *impose* a grand strategy on your team or your organization. Collaboration creates unity, courage, and enthusiasm. Ask God for a vision, and then take time to bring people along. Ask for their candid assessment, invite their input on challenges and opportunities, and involve them in the planning process. When people inevitably get off track, bring them back to the vision and outcomes. Being a defibrillator (especially when no one else sees the need for one) is a leadership challenge, but not as daunting a challenge as leading when momentum is ebbing away.

THINK ABOUT IT:

1) As you look at the S-curve, where is your organization in the growth cycle?

2) What kind of resistance can you expect (from your own inertia and your leaders) if you share a new vision that propels the organization into a period of uncertainty and change?

3) Will it be worth the hassle? Why or why not?

Tailoring Your Voice

4) If you were a consultant, what questions would you ask yourself?

5) How would you answer them?

6) What steps do you need to take to future-proof your organization and yourself?

THE VOICE IN YOUR HEAD BECOMES THE VOICE IN YOUR MOUTH. THE VOICE IN YOUR MOUTH BECOMES THE VOICE IN OTHERS' HEADS.

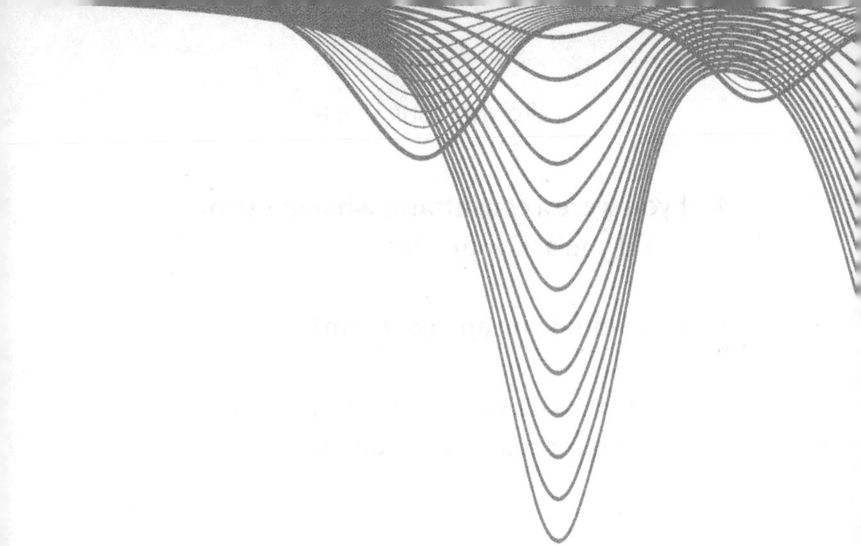

CHAPTER 10

Use Your Voice for Good

WE ARE IN THE MIDDLE OF THE MOST ASTOUNDING acceleration of communication the world has ever known. In only a few decades, pay phones have vanished from airports, letters are seldom mailed, and in-depth research requires only a few clicks instead of countless hours in the library. We can be instantly in touch with billions of people and millions of websites.

VOICES: The Power, Pain, & Purpose of Voices

It's easy to feel overwhelmed by the onslaught of change, and the pace, if anything, is getting even faster.

Virtually all of us have tapped into these new resources to connect with our people. We use email and direct messaging, we create YouTube videos and podcasts, we put our messages online so people can learn and worship anytime and anywhere, we don't have to wait to get in touch with people on our teams, and we have a world of research for our message prep at our fingertips. We've become, at least to a large degree, masters of new technology, but AI, artificial intelligence, is opening new doors to an exciting and challenging future, and we have no idea where it will take us.

After the recent global events, we've come back strong. Our numbers are up, we're reaching more people, and our finances have returned to stability. In the whirlwind of recovering from a couple of years of crisis management, learning to use technology in new ways, and seeing God grow our churches, it's tempting to take a breather . . . a long breather. After all, we've earned it. We deserve it. But as leadership experts point out, "Success breeds complacency, complacency breeds failure." They say, "Becoming a successful CEO [or senior leader] is hard, but staying successful is even harder." For example, within fifteen years, more than half of one year's Fortune 500 companies went bankrupt, were acquired, or ceased to exist.[46] In times of success, our voices of vision, hope, faith, and love need to be clearer and stronger than ever.

THE VOICE OF VISION

What does the voice of vision sound like? Leaders who continually communicate with a powerful, attractive, visionary voice...

Create a cohesive culture.

They value the contributions of each person. As Paul described the body of Christ, those who are often overlooked deserve "greater honor":

The eye cannot say to the hand, "I don't need you!" And the head cannot say to the feet, "I don't need you!" On the contrary, those parts of the body that seem to be weaker are indispensable, and the parts that we think are less honorable we treat with special honor. And the parts that are unpresentable are treated with special modesty, while our presentable parts need no special treatment. But God has put the body together, giving greater honor to the parts that lacked it, so that there should be no division in the body, but that its parts should have equal concern for each other. If one part suffers, every part suffers with it; if

VOICES: The Power, Pain, & Purpose of Voices

one part is honored, every part rejoices with it.
—1 Corinthians 12:21-26

Before you start a meeting, take a minute to mentally scan the room. Identify those who are often overlooked but are faithful, and when the meeting starts, talk about what their contributions mean to you, the team, and the organization.

> Healthy, respectful disagreements often surface new and more effective ideas.

On the other hand, a cohesive culture isn't one that never has tension or conflict; it's one that has learned to address relational problems with wisdom, grace, and truth. Yes, it's uncomfortable, and yes, it takes time, but trust is the glue in any relationship, and strained or broken trust kills the culture. Healthy, respectful disagreements often surface new and more effective ideas. When you sense disagreement is on the horizon, it might be smart to preface the discussion by saying,

Use Your Voice for Good

"I want us to disagree agreeably. After all, we want the same outcomes of people encouraged, our work done well, and God honored. Let's start there and see where our conversation takes us."

Celebrate creativity.
God made us inherently creative. We express it differently, but each of us is created in the image of the God of infinite creativity.

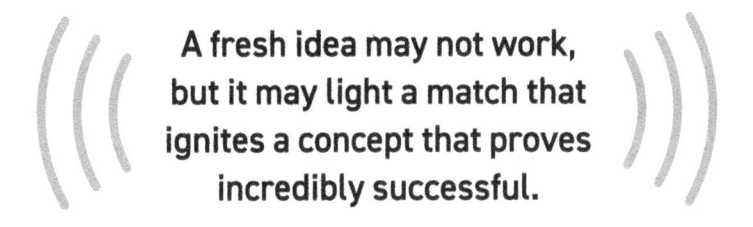

> **A fresh idea may not work, but it may light a match that ignites a concept that proves incredibly successful.**

Secure leaders never respond to an idea by saying, "That just won't work," or "That's not the way we do things around here." A fresh idea may not work, but it may light a match that ignites a concept that proves incredibly successful. And if a creative idea doesn't instantly fit with existing programs and policies, it doesn't mean it's wrong or irrelevant. Good leaders

VOICES: The Power, Pain, & Purpose of Voices

respond, "Tell me more of what you're thinking," and they listen. The act of listening—whether the innovative concept is implemented, altered, or put on the shelf—affirms the person and tells the team that you celebrate their creativity.

Renovate systems.

The policies, procedures, and people who got you *here* aren't necessarily the ones who will get you *there*.

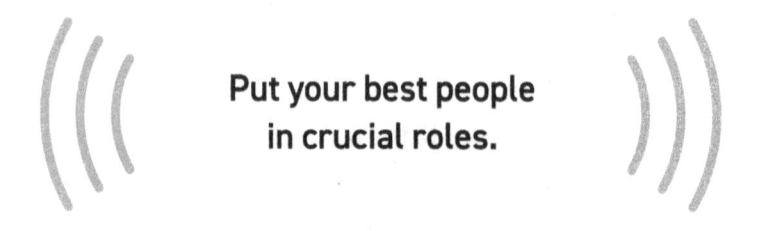

> Put your best people in crucial roles.

We tend to have tunnel vision—seeing that the only possibilities are the ones we've already been implementing. During the period of uncertainty, chaos, and imminent change, analyze what's working well, what's barely adequate, and what's holding you back. Talk to people who have had the courage to make necessary changes, read books and articles, and carefully plan the transitions. Put your best people in crucial roles, including those who are new to the revamped system.

Use Your Voice for Good

You may uncover passions and skills in your people you had no idea existed.

Have a voice that blends boldness and humility.

Not one or the other, but both. Some leaders are bold but not humble—they lead by impressing people with their talents and sometimes intimidating them so they get their way. Other leaders are humble but not bold—they're approachable and kind, but their people are confused by the lack of clear direction. In an article taken from his book, *Good to Great*, Jim Collins explains that his team of researchers were surprised by the qualities in the very best leaders they studied. They called them "Level 5 Leaders." Collins notes:

Level 5 leaders are a study in duality: modest and willful, shy and fearless. To grasp this concept, consider Abraham Lincoln, who never let his ego get in the way of his ambition to create an enduring great nation. Author Henry Adams called him 'a quiet, peaceful, shy figure.' But those who thought Lincoln's understated manner signaled weakness in the man found themselves terribly mistaken— to the scale of 250,000 Confederate and 360,000 Union lives, including Lincoln's own. It might be a stretch to compare the 11 Level 5 CEOs in our research to Lincoln, but they did display the same kind of duality."

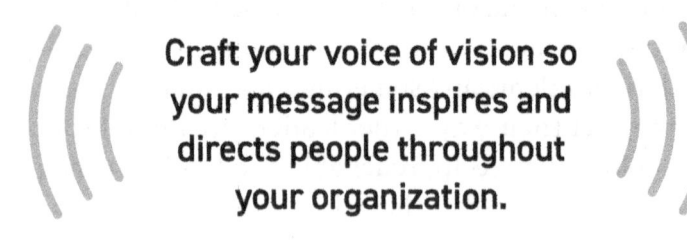

> **Craft your voice of vision so your message inspires and directs people throughout your organization.**

Collins' team identified the powerful blend as "personal humility and professional will." The duality includes:

- » Personal humility: Demonstrates a compelling modesty, shunning public adulation, never boastful.
- » Professional will: Creates superb results, a clear catalyst in the transition from good to great.
- » Personal humility: Acts with quiet, calm determination; relies principally on inspired standards, not inspiring charisma, to motivate.
- » Professional will: Demonstrates an unwavering resolve to do whatever must be done to produce the best long-term results, no matter how difficult.[47]

Even if I've never met you, I know you want to be that kind of leader—or you wouldn't have read this far in the book! Craft your voice of vision so your message inspires and directs people throughout your organization.

YOUR VOICE MATTERS

I'm always amazed at the power of words. In the opening lines of the Bible, we see that everything, "all that is," exists because "God said..." His words separated light from darkness, created matter from nothing, and brought order to chaos. Our words can't bring a universe into existence, but they still have awesome power. Solomon reminds us, "The tongue has the power of life and death, and those who love it will eat its fruit" (Proverbs 18:21). James, the half-brother of Jesus, explained that grace in action requires that we use our voices for good. He describes its power:

When we put bits into the mouths of horses to make them obey us, we can turn the whole animal. Or take ships as an example. Although they are so large and are driven by strong winds, they are steered by a very small rudder wherever the pilot wants to go. Likewise, the tongue is a small part of the body, but it makes great boasts."

VOICES: The Power, Pain, & Purpose of Voices

And he warns,
> *Consider what a great forest is set on fire by a small spark. The tongue also is a fire, a world of evil among the parts of the body. It corrupts the whole body, sets the whole course of one's life on fire, and is itself set on fire by hell.... It is a restless evil, full of deadly poison*—James 3:3-6, 8

We need God's wisdom to use our voices for good. James reminds us, "But the wisdom that comes from heaven is first of all pure; then peace-loving, considerate, submissive, full of mercy and good fruit, impartial and sincere. Peacemakers who sow in peace reap a harvest of righteousness" (James 3:17-18).

Our words and hearts are closely connected and affect each other. In one passage, James says that the condition of our hearts determines the words that come from our mouths, and in another, he says that our words recoil back and affect our hearts. So, we need to be aware that the messages that come from our lips demonstrate what's really going on inside us, yet we have the authority and responsibility to choose our words.

Throughout this book, we've looked at three audiences for our voices:

Use Your Voice for Good

1) We hear voices from within—sometimes conflicting voices of the affirming Holy Spirit and the harsh inner critic.
2) We share our voice with others, hopefully to build them up.
3) We speak the voice of vision and hope over our families, our friends, our congregations, and our communities.

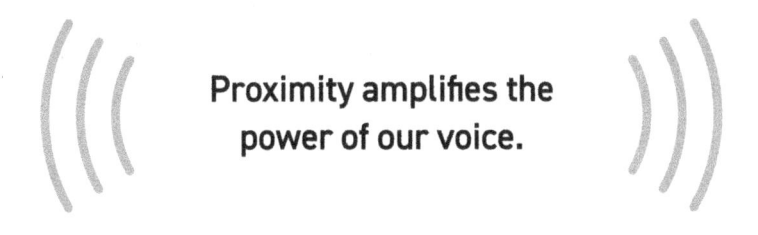

> **Proximity amplifies the power of our voice.**

Proximity amplifies the power of our voice. We can't be close to everyone, but we need to make our voice count with those in our inner circle. The three most powerful messages I've ever been told, and the ones I try to speak to others, are:

1) "I love you,"
2) "I believe in you," and
3) "I'll be there for you."

I've had the great pleasure to speak words of hope and confidence into others' lives, one of whom seemed

VOICES: The Power, Pain, & Purpose of Voices

like a most unlikely recipient. When I was president of Beulah Heights Bible College, Benson Karanja was hired as a janitor, a role that is almost always taken for granted and the person overlooked. But I saw something in Benson, so I introduced him to other executives and gave him honor in their eyes. I enlarged his world by connecting him to people outside his comfort zone. Everyone stands under the same sky, but not all have the same horizon. I wanted to give Benson a much wider, grander vision of what he could become. He began to gain confidence. His optimism, humility, dedication, and intelligence impressed me in every interaction. I promoted him from janitor to library assistant, to head librarian, to accountant as one of our administrators, to professor, to director of student affairs, to vice president, to executive vice president, and finally, to president of the college. During these stages, he studied hard and earned multiple degrees.

From the beginning, I observed Benson's powerfully positive impact on others. It didn't take long to develop a glowing opinion of him, and over the years, this opinion grew even stronger. At every turn, I looked for opportunities for him to have a broader, deeper impact on the faculty, staff, and students. I opened a lot of doors for him because he earned my trust and confidence.

Use Your Voice for Good

MY VOICE TO ALL LEADERS

In the summer of 1980, I had just been selected as the pastor of my first church in Hartford, Michigan, a little town with one red light. Soon after Brenda and I moved in, I went to our denomination's regional conference in Ohio. The leader of the conference was Bishop Chester Miller, a highly respected man who had been a missionary in Brazil. He was soft-spoken, and his demeanor was gentle. At one point between meetings, I saw him across the campus. I ran over to him and said excitedly, "Bishop Miller, have you heard? I've just been elected as the pastor of a church in Hartford, Michigan!"

> "Brother Sam, live long, live clean."

He smiled and told me, "Yes, Brother Sam. I heard the news. Congratulations."

VOICES: The Power, Pain, & Purpose of Voices

I was ready to hear some deep, godly wisdom. I could hardly contain myself. "Bishop Miller, if you could give me one piece of advice, what would it be?"

I fully expected him to give me God's direction for my life and ministry, maybe start this program or learn from that leader. But when he spoke, I was deeply disappointed. There, on the hot sidewalk, as we stood in the August sun, he didn't even look me in the eye when he said softly, "Brother Sam, live long, live clean." He walked away.

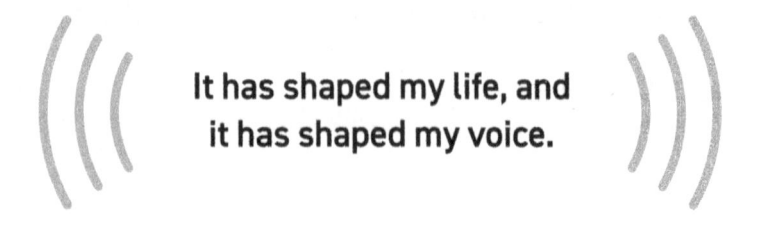

> **It has shaped my life, and it has shaped my voice.**

At that moment, I thought his advice was mud, but over the years, I've found it to be pure gold. When I'm tempted, I hear the voice of Bishop Chester Miller. When it would be easier to cut corners on my preparation for a talk, I hear the voice of Bishop Miller. When there's an opportunity to overlook an ethical consideration, I hear the Bishop's voice. When others are gossiping and I want to join in, I hear Bishop Miller's voice. "Live long, live clean." The conversation at the conference lasted only a minute, and it happened decades ago, but I remember it like it was yesterday. It has shaped my life, and it has shaped my voice.

What voices are making a difference in you today? Which ones speak life, and which ones speak death?

What is your voice in the lives of those around you? You have the high privilege and deep responsibility to use your voice for good. What are you saying to "warn those who are idle and disruptive, encourage the disheartened, help the weak, be patient with everyone" (1 Thessalonians 5:14)? Each moment is a God-ordained opportunity to use your voice to bring hope to the hopeless and challenge to those eager to make a difference.

Most importantly, who needs to hear your voice?

THINK ABOUT IT:

1) What are you doing well, and what can you improve as you use your voice to:
   » Create a cohesive culture?
   » Celebrate creativity?
   » Blend boldness and humility?

VOICES: The Power, Pain, & Purpose of Voices

2) Whose voices do you need to listen to more closely?

3) Whose voices do you need to ignore or refute?

4) What are two or three specific applications you want to make from this book?

THE VOICE IN YOUR HEAD BECOMES THE VOICE IN YOUR MOUTH. THE VOICE IN YOUR MOUTH BECOMES THE VOICE IN OTHERS' HEADS.

Endnotes

1 Jessica Golden, "Pickleball popularity exploded last year, with more than 36 million playing the sport," *CNBC*, 5 January 2023, https://www.cnbc.com/2023/01/05/pickleball-popularity-explodes-with-more-than-36-million-playing.html.
2 "You Never Know When a Moment and a Few Sincere Words Can Have an Impact on a Life Forever," *Ziglar.com*, https://www.ziglar.com/quotes/you-never-know/.
3 Lori Harris, "Cognitive Communication: Communicating to Maximize Excellence and Business Results," *Forbes*, 5 January 2022, https://www.forbes.com/sites/forbescoachescouncil/2022/01/05/cognitive-communication-communicating-to-maximize-excellence-and-business-results/?sh=75076d6d13a1.
4 Jobs, Steve. "Stay Hungry. Stay Foolish." Stanford Commencement Address, 2005, https://fs.blog/steve-jobs-stanford-commencement/.
5 Sam Chand, *How Leaders Create Chaos: And Why They Should* (Sanford, FL: AVAIL, December 27, 2022).
6 Michelle Woods Waldron, "Voices."
7 Pete Walker, "Shrinking the Inner Critic in Complex PTSD," *Pete Walker*, https://pete-walker.com/shrinkingInnerCritic.htm.
8 Brené Brown, *I Thought It Was Just Me (But It Isn't): Making the Journey from "What Will People Think?" to "I Am Enough"* (New York, NY: Avery, February 1, 2007), 27.
9 Brené Brown, *Daring Greatly: How the Courage to Be Vulnerable Transforms the Way We Live, Love, Parent, and Lead* (New York, NY: Avery: April 7, 2015), 58.

VOICES: The Power, Pain, & Purpose of Voices

10 "NASA Research Illuminates Medical Uses of Light," *NASA*, 19 May 2022, https://spinoff.nasa.gov/NASA-Research-Illuminates-Medical-Uses-of-Light.

11 Leonardo Blair, "With Rising Discontent, More than Half of American clergy seriously considered quitting: study," *Christian Post*, 11 January 2024, https://www.christianpost.com/news/over-half-of-american-pastors-have-considered-quitting-poll.html.

12 Rita McGrath, "Transient Advantage" post, *LinkedIn*, https://www.linkedin.com/posts/ritamcgrath_can-your-career-survive-transient-competitive-activity-7103461234808606720-OG_o.

13 Adapted from Dr. Travis Bradberry, "Six Toxic Thoughts Successful People Quarantine" post, *LinkedIn*, 11 December 2017, https://www.linkedin.com/pulse/six-toxic-thoughts-successful-people-quarantine-dr-travis-bradberry.

14 Jethro Nededog, "Oprah says every guest asks her the same question after their interviews—but she was still shocked when Beyoncé asked it," *Business Insider*, 25 September 2017, https://www.businessinsider.com/oprah-winfrey-question-every-guests-asks-after-interviews-beyonce-2017-9.

15 Cited in *Summa Theologica* by Thomas Aquinas, https://www.ccel.org/ccel/aquinas/summa.SS_Q158_A8.html.

16 Martin Marty, *A Cry of Absence: Reflections for the Winter of the Heart* (New York, NY: Harper & Row, 1983), p. 39.

17 Amy Rees Anderson, "The Fastest Way to Achieve Success Is to First Help Others Succeed," *Forbes*, 6 January 2016, https://www.forbes.com/sites/amyanderson/2016/01/06/the-fastest-way-to-achieve-success-is-to-first-help-others-succeed/?sh=33e025b879f9.

18 T. R. Witcher, "From Disaster to Prevention: The Silver Bridge," *Civil Engineering Magazine* 87, no. 11 (December 2017): 45, https://doi.org/10.1061/ciegag.0001250.

19 Adapted from Thom Ranier, https://churchanswers.com/blog/nine-microstresses-of-a-pastor/

20 Ernest Hemingway, *The Sun Also Rises* (New York, NY: Vintage, January 5, 2022), 141.

Endnotes

21 "The Man, the Boy, and the Donkey," Aesop's Fables, *Lit2Go*, cited at https://etc.usf.edu/lit2go/35/aesops-fables/648/the-man-the-boy-and-the-donkey/.

22 John Huston, *The Bible* (September 28, 1966; Los Angeles, CA: Twentieth Century-Fox Film Corporation).

23 Nadia, "How Many Ads Do We See a Day?", *Siteefy*, 25 April 2024, https://siteefy.com/how-many-ads-we-see-a-day/.

24 Ivan Blagojević, "Texting Statistics," *99Firms*, https://99firms.com/blog/texting-statistics/#gref.

25 Blagojević, "Texting Statistics."

26 Emma Seppälä and Kim Cameron, "The Best Leaders Have a Contagious Positive Energy," *Harvard Business Review*, 18 April 2022, https://hbr.org/2022/04/the-best-leaders-have-a-contagious-positive-energy.

27 Joe Iarocci, "15 Great Quotes about Questioning," post, *LinkedIn*, 6 June 2016, https://www.linkedin.com/pulse/15-great-quotes-questioning-joe-iarocci.

28 Adapted from Carolyn Dewar et al., "Staying ahead: How the best CEOs continually improve performance," *McKinsey & Company*, 25 May 2023, https://www.mckinsey.com/capabilities/strategy-and-corporate-finance/our-insights/staying-ahead-how-the-best-ceos-continually-improve-performance.

29 "A New Chapter in Millennial Church Attendance," *Barna*, 4 August 2022, https://www.barna.com/research/church-attendance-2022/.

30 "People Who Are Good at Dealing with Conflict Ask This 1 Question, Says a Harvard Communications Expert," *Inc.*, 9 November 2023, https://www.inc.com/minda-zetlin/people-who-are-good-at-dealing-with-conflict-always-ask-this-1-question-says-harvard-communication-expert.html/

31 Martin Zwilling, "9 Communication Principles for Today's Business Leaders," *Inc.*, 16 May 2024, https://www.inc.com/martin-zwilling/9-communication-principles-for-todays-business-leaders.html.

32 Cited in Erik Larson, "Why Decision-Making Needs to Top Your 2022 Growth Agenda," *Forbes*, 8 September 2021, https://www.forbes.com/sites/eriklarson/2021/09/08/why-decision-making-needs-to-top-your-2022-growth-agenda/?sh=122006f8282f.

VOICES: The Power, Pain, & Purpose of Voices

33   Anna Baluch, "What Is the S-Curve in Project Management?" *Forbes*, 7 June 2023, https://www.forbes.com/advisor/business/s-curve/.

34   Christine Kininmonth, "Detailed Summary of CEO Excellence by McKinsey & Company Senior Partners," *The Growth Faculty*, 28 September 2022, https://thegrowthfaculty.com/articles/CEOExcellenceMckinsey/?ref=charterworks.com.

35   Kininmonth, "Detailed Summary."

36   Daniel Kahneman, *Thinking, Fast and Slow* (New York, NY: Farrar, Straus and Giroux, April 2, 2013).

37   Luis Velasquez and Kristin Gleitsman, "6 Ways to Become a More Collaborative Leader," *Harvard Business Review*, 10 July 2023, https://hbr.org/2023/07/6-ways-to-become-a-more-collaborative-leader.

38   "Staying Ahead: How the Best CEOs Continually Improve Performance," *McKinsey & Company*, 25 May 2023, https://www.mckinsey.com/capabilities/strategy-and-corporate-finance/our-insights/staying-ahead-how-the-best-ceos-continually-improve-performance.

39   "Staying Ahead," *McKinsey & Company*.

40   Richard S. Tedlow, "The Education of Andy Grove," *Fortune*, 21 March 2016, https://fortune.com/2016/03/21/andy-grove-fortune-classic/.

41   Jim Collins, *Good to Great: Why Some Companies Make the Leap … And Others Don't* (New York, NY: Harper Business, October 16, 2001).

42   Nick Hobson, "Warren Buffett: There Are Successful People and Really Successful People. What Separates the Two, *Inc.*, 31 May 2023, https://www.inc.com/nick-hobson/warren-buffett-there-are-successful-people-really-successful-people-what-separates-two.html.

43   Adapted from Carey Nieuwhof, "7 Things that get harder as your church grows," *Carey Nieuwhof Blog*, https://careynieuwhof.com/7-things-that-get-harder-as-your-church-grows/.

44   Josh Katzowitz, "Top Ten Super Bowl-winning coaches who eventually got fired," *CBS Sports*, 12 December 2023, https://www.cbssports.com/nfl/news/top-ten-super-bowl-winning-coaches-who-eventually-got-fired/.

Endnotes

45 Dewar et al., "Staying ahead."
46 Dewar et al., "Staying ahead."
47 Jim Collins, "Level 5 Leadership: The Triumph of Humility and Fierce Resolve," *Harvard Business Review*, 1 January 2001, https://hbr.org/2001/01/level-5-leadership-the-triumph-of-humility-and-fierce-resolve-2.

PAY *WHATEVER* YOU CAN!

WE WILL LET YOU SET YOUR OWN TUITION PRICE.

Amazing things happen when a group of like-minded, high-achieving and diverse leaders gather with one goal in mind: to succeed like never before. The Sam Chand Leadership Institute is a place where you can network, learn and be empowered to reach your potential and see success in your life's work.

Leadership is a journey, and you don't have to take it alone! If you're tired of the status quo and are ready to go to a whole new level, you're in the right place.

TO DATE WE HAVE GIVEN AWAY $5 MILLION IN FINANCIAL AID

SAM CHAND
LEADERSHIP INSTITUTE

CHECK OUT OFFER AT
SAMCHANDLEADERSHIPOFFER.COM

AVAIL+

TRY FOR 30 DAYS *AND RECEIVE*
THE SEQUENCE TO SUCCESS
BUNDLE *FREE*

$79 VALUE

+ BOOK
+ STUDY GUIDE
+ ONLINE COURSE
+ LIVE CLASS
+ MORE

The Art *of* Leadership

This isn't just another leadership collective...this is the next level of networking, resources, and empowerment designed specifically for leaders like you.

Whether you're an innovator in ministry, business, or your community, **AVAIL+** is designed to take you to your next level. Each one of us needs connection. Each one of us needs practical advice. Each one of us needs inspiration. **AVAIL+** is all about equipping you, so that you can turn around and equip those you lead.

THEARTOFLEADERSHIP.COM/CHAND

AVAIL
The ART of LEADERSHIP

CLAIM YOUR *FREE* ANNUAL SUBSCRIPTION

FreeAvailOffer.com
To claim your subscription ($59 value)

SCAN HERE TO LEARN MORE

THE AVAIL PODCAST
HOSTED BY VIRGIL SIERRA

AVAIL
PODCAST

FOLLOW THE LEADER

STAY CONNECTED

facebook.com/TheArtofAvail   @theartofavail   AVAIL